QUESTIONS
THAT GET
RESULTS

INNOVATIVE IDEAS
MANAGERS CAN USE TO
IMPROVE THEIR
TEAMS' PERFORMANCE

PAUL CHERRY

PATRICK CONNOR

WITH

KARIANNE
EARNER-SPARKS

WILEY

John Wiley & Sons, Inc.

For general information on our other products and services or for technical support, please contact our Customer Care Department within the United States at (800) 762-2974, outside the United States at (317) 572-3993 or fax (317) 572-4002.

Wiley also publishes its books in a variety of electronic formats. Some content that appears in print may not be available in electronic books. For more information about Wiley products, visit our web site at www.wiley.com.

ISBN 978-0-470-76784-9 (paper)
ISBN 978-0-470-92554-6 (ebk)
ISBN 978-0-470-92555-3 (ebk)
ISBN 978-0-470-92556-0 (ebk)

Printed in the United States of America

10 9 8 7 6 5 4 3 2 1

Contents

Contents

Introduction

Why did we write *Questions That Get Results?* Simply, because we see thousands of dedicated, hard-working businesspeople each year who are eager to be successful, but sometimes lack certain skills to enhance their job performance. We are fortunate that companies ask us to come and coach their managers in areas such as delegation, motivation, team building, and developing client relationships, as this gives us a unique opportunity to meet wonderful professionals every year and to make a real difference in their careers. The problem is, usually we do not get to spend as much time as we would like with individual managers. We have so many tools we would like to share with them, but too often we are given a strictly limited amount of time to do that. To address that dilemma, we decided to compile in a book the problems and issues that most managers commonly face, along with the answers to those problems, so that this valuable information would be easily accessible to everyone.

What is our message? Good management can make or break a company. We have personally witnessed unbelievable turnarounds by managers who used their considerable skills to alter company culture, drastically improve employee motivation, effectively restructure departments, and/or create the opportunity to forge lasting client relationships. Conversely, we have seen solid companies brought to their knees by managers who acted like tyrants, neglected their responsibilities, resisted change, and, predictably, caused their organizations to fail. What we have learned from these experiences is that good management comes down to effective communication. That is why we have chosen to focus on the questions in this book. By asking the right questions, you, as a manager, can start dialogues and solve problems, seize opportunities, and create a more successful team—which is why the subtitle of our book is *Innovative Ideas Managers Can Use to Improve Their Teams' Performance*. Being a great manager is not about catchphrases, strategic plans, or quotas. Great management results from engaging in purposeful interactions between you and your employees, you and your counterparts, you and your supervisors, you and your clients—even you and yourself.

Who is our target reader? Anyone in a management position will benefit from the skills taught in this book. It does not matter if you are just starting out in your career or have spent the last 25 years in a management role. Regardless of whether you were trained to be a manager or have recently been promoted to management in a specialized skill area, such as engineering or nursing, you will find concrete, sensible guidance in these pages. The advice we give will be helpful to managers universally.

What will you gain from this book? You will build an arsenal of tools you can use to improve your team's productivity. You will learn how to use questions to coach and motivate your employees, to delegate responsibilities to them, and to build a highly effective and cohesive department in your company. You will also learn how to use questions to improve your working relationships with your colleagues.

We dedicate a chapter to questions you can use when faced with an uncooperative colleague or unproductive department; there is also a chapter on how to use questions to manage those above you. Primarily, though, you will find several chapters dedicated to *you*. One addresses how to use questions to manage your career; another provides you with questions to ask when evaluating a potential job opportunity.

What results can you expect from this book? One of the most rewarding uses of these tools is that they will allow you to spend your time being proactive, rather than reactive. Many managers fall into the trap of going from one problem to another, "putting out fires," leaving them little or no time to address the underlying issues. Furthermore, they spend so much time focusing on what is going wrong in the present that they have little time left for future planning or developing goals. One major benefit of following our advice, then, is that you will have much more time for these forward-thinking activities. By creating a truly effective team—one that works together to address problems on its own—and learning to delegate, coach, and motivate that team, we assure you that the number of fires you will have to put out will be fewer and farther between. In sum, you will find yourself in a happier workplace, one marked by smoother interactions between employees, managers, executives, and clients alike.

Once you have taken the immediate problems off of your plate, you will be able to gain insight into what you want for your future, both professionally and personally. So, we also give you the steps you will need to take in order to get there. Spending a small amount of time taking stock of your professional life will keep you from wasting years pursuing goals that are out of sync with your true desires. Not only will you determine what you want out of your career, but you will also ensure that you have the skills and qualifications you need to achieve those goals.

Let us be clear: We are not offering quick fixes here. Being a manager can be an extremely difficult and, at times, thankless job. What we do offer you are tools—in the form of questions—that will get you through the difficult times and help to ensure you will have more of the better times in the future.

After many years of working with businesspeople, we are optimistic that the vast majority want to do their jobs well. As a manager, it is your job to tap into that desire and create success for yourself and all those around you. *Questions That Get Results* can help you do that.

CHAPTER 1

Questions That Get Results

Have you ever been in a meeting where the participants ramble on, talking over and around the topic(s) on the agenda, and the conversation goes nowhere? Usually in this situation, one of two things will happen. You will either be lucky enough to have an effective manager who will step in early and ask the right questions that lead everyone to the heart of the issue, or you will be cursed with a bad manager who lets the rambling go on and on before he or she eventually says, "Okay, we have to move on now."

Commonly, people believe that the ability of highly qualified managers to ask the right questions at the right time is an innate skill, something that cannot be taught. In fact, such managers prepare in advance. They spend time learning which questions to ask and when and how to apply them appropriately to each new situation. They craft pertinent, relevant questions long before they have a need to use them. Great managers develop their skill sets so that they can motivate, coach, cut through the fluff, and hold people accountable. Utilizing the right questions at the right time helps them do that.

Patrick once attended a board meeting at which one of the participants had been talking around a problem for 45 long, tedious minutes. Then, another board member arrived late and joined the discussion. He asked two or three pointed questions that immediately uncovered the causes of the problem and offered several possible solutions. Not only did he mercifully end the other board member's monologue, he also successfully steered the discussion from the problem stage to the solution stage. Who knows what would have happened if he had not been able to make it to the meeting? Patrick might still be sitting there, listening to the long-winded board member go on and on.

Throughout this chapter, we will discuss several types of questions that can be used to get better results, whether for the purpose of focusing a discussion, weeding out an unproductive team member, identifying the issue, holding up the implementation of an important plan, or revealing an executive's criteria for success.

USING QUESTIONS TO SOLVE PROBLEMS

There will be occasions and circumstances when what you have to tell others is not in line with what they want to hear. For example, let's say you face the challenge of presenting a new idea to your employees; obviously, you have a lot to lose if you go about it the wrong way, especially if the idea is controversial or apt to cause discontent among the ranks. Sometimes the best way to make sure a new concept is accepted is to ask your employees their opinion on it *before* unveiling the full-blown plan to them. Employees usually know what they need in order to get their jobs done; therefore, they are in a better position than anyone else to know how a new plan or product will help or hinder their work. Your challenge, then, is to ask specific questions that will get them thinking hard about exactly what they need, as opposed to asking generic questions that will surely yield only generic responses.

In our research, we have found that managers tend to ask the same questions of their employees, regardless of the industry.

These questions are often well intentioned, but garner little useful information:

- "How's it going?"
- "What's happening?"
- "How are you coming along with _____ (the project, task, job, customer, etc.)?"
- "Do you have any questions?"
- "When can I expect _____?"
- "What do you need?"
- "What do you have for me?"
- "Is there anything I need to know?"
- "How'd you like that _____ (meeting, training, information, person, etc.)?"
- "Why don't you touch base if anything comes up?"
- "How can I help?"

The problem with most of these questions is that because they're vague, employees tend to give vague answers, containing little or no substance. Unless an employee is self-motivated to open up to a manager, these questions will not provide insight into an individual's true state of mind or the very real issues he or she might be facing.

For example, let us look at the last question: "How can I help?" On the surface, it sounds like a good open-ended question. If an employee is having difficulty at work and is asked that question, he or she might respond with genuine feeling, saying something like, "I have two important deadlines to meet this week, and I know I will not be able to get everything done on time." The trouble is, most of the time a question like "How can I help?" is answered superficially—for example, "Oh, I'm fine, but thanks for the offer." Many employees are unwilling to admit they need help. They are afraid that doing so will convey the message that they are unable to handle their workload. Or they don't believe that their manager's offers to help are genuine. Either way, a generic question like this too often is going to lead to a generic answer, one of no use to anyone.

DESCRIPTIVE QUESTIONS

One of the best ways to ask questions is to use what we call "descriptive openers." These are phrases that can initiate dialogue and motivate people to open up. Using these phrases makes it possible to craft questions that elicit as much information as possible. In the sample questions here, the descriptive phrases are in bold:

- "Can you **take me through** each step of the process you have implemented so far?"
- "Will you please **describe for me** how you think we could improve this process?"
- "Can you **clarify for me** how this idea will meet our requirements?"
- "Will you please **share with me** which systems, programs, or people are helpful, and which are a hindrance?"
- "Can you **explain to me** what has transpired so far?"
- "Will you please **help me understand** your thoughts on this project?"
- "Can you **walk me through** your timetable for implementing these changes?"

The best way to illustrate the effectiveness of these questions is by example. In the first scenario, Kristin, the manager, uses generic questions to ask an employee about meeting a deadline. In the second, she uses descriptive questions to garner much more information.

Kristin: Sheila, I was wondering how things are going with the Schofield project?

Sheila: Everything is going fine.

Kristin: Can I help you with that at all?

Sheila: Thanks, but I've got it under control.

Kristin: Okay, so I can expect it on my desk on Thursday?

Sheila: Yup, that is not a problem.

Now, coming away from this exchange, Kristin would probably feel as if she were doing a good job, checking in with Sheila and making sure everything is going according to schedule. She might even pat herself on the back for offering to help and confirming the Thursday deadline. The problem with these questions, however, is that Kristin did not obtain any actual information from Sheila as to the status of the project. All she knows is that, according to Sheila, everything is "fine."

Now let's see how this situation might play out when Kristin uses descriptive questions, which are again highlighted in bold.

Kristin: Sheila, I want to talk to you about the Schofield project. I know it is really complex and that there are a lot of pieces to put together. I'm checking in to see how things are going. Can you **take me through** each step of the process you have implemented so far?

Sheila: Well, I have amassed all of the research and now I am waiting for the summaries from my assistants.

Kristin: Okay. Have you written up the five-point plan yet?

Sheila: Well, actually, I have not because, as I said, I am waiting for the summaries.

Kristin: Can you **take me through** your timetable for implementing these changes?

Sheila: As soon as I have the summaries, I can write the five-point plan.

Kristin: Will you **help me understand** how it is you are sure that the project will be ready by the deadline, considering that the Legal Department needs three to five days to review the plan after you have written it?

Sheila: I guess I didn't budget time for Legal into my plan.

Kristin: Can you **explain to me** how that happened?

Sheila: I think two things happened. One, I needed my assistants to summarize the research, but they were busy helping Fran with her project, which was due last week. Even though I gave them the task to complete, I did not specify a time frame for when it had to be done. Two, it has been a while since I worked on a project that needed approval from Legal. I guess I forgot how much lead time I had to give them.

As Sheila's manager, Kristin would obviously feel quite differently about this exchange than the one in the first scenario. Note that the situations are the same; it is only the information gathered by the manager that is different. As a result of using descriptive questions, Kristin discovers the true state of the project and can then offer the assistance Sheila clearly needs to finish the project on time.

Descriptive openers such as these strongly encourage whoever is being asked the questions to give substantive answers. In the past, many of us were taught to ask questions that started with "who," "what," "where," "when," "why," and "how." These interrogatives have their use, of course, but too often they allow the respondent to be evasive, if that is his or her intent. Here are some examples of what appear to be good questions, followed by the unsatisfactory answers they tend to elicit:

Question: Who do you have working on this project?
Answer: Oh, I have the whole team working on it.

Question: What do you need to get this finished?
Answer: I have everything I need. I have it covered.

Question: Where are the specs I need?
Answer: I am almost done with them.

Question: When can I expect that report on my desk?
Answer: Any day now.

Question: Why have you missed your deadline?
Answer: I have been really busy; it won't happen again.

Question: How are things going on this project?
Answer: Things are going great.

As you can see, even a well-intentioned manager who is genuinely interested in what is going on with his or her employees might not get worthwhile information by asking these questions. That is why we suggest using descriptive openers when asking many different types of questions (see below for examples). They demand more from the respondent than other types of openers.

COMPARE-AND-CONTRAST QUESTIONS

Asking compare-and-contrast questions is an effective way to learn more about your employees, your counterparts, and the top executives at your company. They also enable you to uncover how preferences and needs change over time and which factors are most important to decision makers.

Compare-and-contrast questions use words and phrases such as the following:

- Differ
- Compare
- Versus
- Evolve
- Rank from most important to least
- Oppose
- Contrast

Throughout this section, we describe several types of situations where compare-and-contrast questions work best. These include: managing internal relationships, implementing change over time, and determining criteria. We'll look first at how compare-and-contrast questions can improve internal relationships.

Managing Internal Relationships

Among the most delicate issues that managers have to address are those involving internal company politics. Whether the issue at hand is as complicated as a merger or layoffs, or as simple as planning a company picnic, unintentionally "stepping on toes" at the office will get you into trouble every time. To avoid this, we recommend that you begin by asking questions of those colleagues with whom you already have a relationship, in order to understand the possible objections or concerns of those with whom you do not. We have found that asking compare-and-contrast questions is a great way of doing this. These questions allow you to poll a number of people to get a feel for a situation *before* you present an idea or plan to a bigger group or the company at large.

Here are some examples. Notice that in many of the samples, we use descriptive openers to help focus the question:

- "Can you clarify for me how your opinion might differ from those of your team members'?"
- "As you take me through the decision-making process for this project, can you explain what is most important, versus what is least important?"
- "Can you share with me your thoughts on how Bill's reaction to this might differ from Terry's?"
- "As you think about the members of the committee, can you tell me your opinion as to who would be the most receptive to this idea and who might be the least receptive?"
- "In your experience, what has been the top concern for Sue, as compared to Jan?"

As you can see, these questions can help you identify attitudes, possible pitfalls, and preferences before you introduce a new plan or suggestion. In our experience as training consultants, we have found that the more we know about our clients, their employees, and their organizations, the better the results will be for them—and for us. We have also learned that when leadership tries to implement change within an organization, the biggest objection from employees usually is: "You don't understand my situation." What this statement really means is: "You do not know my job. You do not realize what I have to deal with on a regular basis, and now you are instituting yet another initiative that will make things more difficult for me on a daily basis."

When employees do not feel understood, they resist change more fiercely. But when they are included in the decision-making process and treated as valued resources, they can be the staunchest champions of new initiatives. As a manager, how do you go about doing this? The best way is to gather input from your employees before you introduce any new plan or initiative. All it takes is the investment of time at the beginning of the process—time to ask the staff specific, targeted questions about problems and potential solutions. Compare-and-contrast questions can help you do this.

Implementing Change over Time

The second problem area compare-and-contrast questions can help you tackle is change over time. As a manager, it is important to keep track of how your team and your company respond to and adapt to change. Chances are, the issues and problems that plagued them this month will be long forgotten by next quarter; likewise, the potential opportunities and areas for growth that present themselves now will be obsolete in six months. That is why you need to be able to ask the questions that can flesh out how change manifests within your organization. Here are some questions that can help you do this:

- "Can you share with me your strategy for addressing this issue? How does that compare with what you did in the past?"
- "Will you tell me how your needs have evolved over the past 12 months?"
- "Can you help me understand the potential opportunities you anticipate arising in the next year? How do they compare with opportunities you have had in the past?"
- "Will you describe for me what you believe differentiates this approach from tactics you have used in the past?"

- "Can you tell me your ideal outcome, and describe how it differs from your current situation?"
- "Will you share with me your goals for this year, versus those from last year?"

Determining Criteria

The last area where you can use compare-and-contrast questions to great advantage is in determining the objectives and criteria of others. It is easy to get into trouble when we assume that whatever is important to us is also important to other people.

For example, consider Tom, a manager who works in sales and is very focused on quotas and revenue, whereas for his colleague, Joan, a manager working in research and development, those items are at the bottom of the priority list. Therefore, when Tom has a new plan, and intends to approach Joan about it, he should not assume that they share the same priorities or goals. Instead, he should ask Joan compare-and-contrast questions to help him discover what's important to Joan. Only after hearing what she has to say should he craft his proposal to address both sets of criteria.

Here are some questions Tom might ask Joan:

- "Can you walk me through the factors that are most important to you when creating a new project, as well as those that are least important?"
- "Will you share with me your top priorities when evaluating a new project?"
- "Can you rank the following criteria in order of importance, from most important to least important: safety, power, quality, and price?"

As you can see, compare-and-contrast questions can be used in a variety of different circumstances. Sometimes, however, the people involved do not appreciate the need for change, in which case you may need to turn to impact questions as a way to get to the core issue.

IMPACT QUESTIONS

Impact questions are crucial because they address motivations, and determine whether or not someone has a sense of urgency about an issue. They can help you figure out if an individual at your company is receptive to change, or sees a problem in the same light as you. If employees are not treating an urgent problem appropriately, impact questions can also be used to help them put things into perspective. This way they can recognize the severity of a situation—and, best of all, they will arrive at this conclusion through their own words by answering your questions.

As an example, imagine you want to implement a change in the way your organization deals with production delays. You're fed up with this situation, and now you've come up with a plan to solve it. This solution, however, will require a great deal of effort on the part of your employees and others in the organization, and all of them are resisting the change. In order to get them to buy into your plan, you need to have your employees and counterparts understand the severity of this problem. Here are several questions you might ask in order to accomplish your goal:

- "If this problem does not get addressed, what kind of impact will it have on our department?"
- "How might this issue affect your department in the long run if it is not solved?"
- "We are losing *X* amount of money each quarter because of this situation. How can we afford *not* to take action?"
- "Let us assume nothing changes: What is it going to cost us in terms of resources, clients, personnel, and output?"
- "What do you think the consequence will be if we continue doing exactly what we're doing now?"

If you can get your employees and counterparts to articulate the gravity of the problem in their own words, the implementation of your plan to fix it will proceed much more smoothly.

LOCK-ON QUESTIONS

As managers, we would like to think we have all the answers. In reality, though, we are sometimes at a loss as to how we should proceed. You might, for example, feel like you are not getting the whole truth from one of your employees; or you might not be sure what is going on with your team. In either case, we recommend using lock-on questions to gain more information and uncover the next step you need to take.

A lock-on question is a very simple tool you can use to learn a lot more when you do not have all the answers, or you think there is something you might be missing. Here is an example when to use the lock-on question:

Your team has not been producing as well as it should. You have followed all of the steps itemized previously but still do not know what is going wrong. You decide to approach the senior member of the team, Alice, to uncover the problem. She tells you, "Things have just been crazy around here." You want to find out more—what "crazy" really means—but Alice seems unwilling or unable to share the details with you. Instead of getting frustrated or feeling at a loss as to where to go next, ask a lock-on question to get to the heart of the issue.

You might say to Alice, "I understand that this month has been very hectic. You usually do such a great job handling the crises in our office, and we really appreciate how hard you work. I noticed you said that things have been 'crazy'; could you elaborate on that?" This compliment combined with a question would serve to make Alice feel more at ease and ready to open up. She might then tell you, "To be honest, Brad and Terry have left the rest of us holding down the fort while they spend 90 percent of their time working on the proposal for our new government contract. I know that proposal is really important, so I didn't want to say anything; but the rest of our team is getting hammered with other work."

Once you know the true nature of the problem, you and Alice and the rest of the team can sit down together and figure out how to solve it.

Team members can be reluctant to bring us problems like these because so many managers respond by saying things like, "Just make it work." In these instances, when our team needs our guidance, it is extremely helpful to have the lock-on question as a tool in our kit.

There are two key parts to the lock-on question:

Part 1, Acknowledge: This part of the lock-on question is very important because you are acknowledging the other person's problem and empathizing with his or her situation. For example, if an employee tells you, "I am just too busy to tackle that right now," you would respond by saying: "I understand how busy you are. I know that you always put in 110 percent and there are never enough hours in the day. It is amazing how much work you can get done."

Part 2, Question: Once you have acknowledged where someone is coming from, you need to follow up with a question that focuses—"locks on"—to a particular part of his or her statement. For example, if a team member tells you, "We have been trying to get that project off of the ground for months," you might lock on to the word "trying" and then phrase a question around it. You might ask, "I noticed you said you have been trying to get it off the ground for months. What has worked for you so far, and what has been holding you back from completing the project?"

CONCLUSION

As a manager, you want to have the answers; you do not want to look stupid—no one does. But you have to empower your people to come up with their own answers. You cannot spend all your time solving everyone else's problems. The beauty of the lock-on question is that it lets you probe the other person's mind for ideas. You are asking him or her to figure out the real issue and why something has not been done about it.

We believe that asking great questions is at the heart of great management. It is not always about knowing all the answers; rather, it is about having the ability and desire to find out the answers. They might come from your counterparts in other departments, the top executives at your company, or your reports. You will only be able to uncover these answers, however, if you know the right questions to ask. Using the guidelines and suggestions we give you throughout this book, we are confident that you, too, will find great value in asking the right questions for every situation.

For more information on topics discussed in this chapter, visit our website at www.questionsthatgetresults.com/results.

CHAPTER 2

Questions That Manage Your Team

A team is more than the sum of its parts. If you have a high-functioning team, it will outperform a more skilled or knowledge-able team that is dysfunctional. You see this happen on sports teams all the time. In 2004, the USA Olympic basketball team was composed of superstars from the NBA, including LeBron James, Allen Iverson, Tim Duncan, and Carmelo Anthony. Despite all of this star power, Team USA came away with a very humbling third place, instead of the expected first-place finish. The American team was defeated by the teams from Lithuania, Argentina, and Puerto Rico, hardly basketball powerhouses. It was widely agreed that although Team USA had far more talent and skill than the other teams, the team itself was dysfunctional, and the egos of the players prevented them from working together effectively. Meanwhile, the Lithuanian, Argentine, and Puerto Rican teams had spent years practicing together, and their ability to function as a unit enabled them to defeat a more highly skilled competitor.

As a manager, your team represents you and your company. Its members are not just employees; they are the face of the company to customers and clients. If your team cannot work together, it is not just their problem; it is yours. If they anger a customer, you have to be the one to step in to resolve the issue. If they miss a deadline, you are responsible. Of course, managers deal with these problems all the time, but wouldn't it be nice if you could prevent some of those problems *before* they occur?

This chapter focuses on how to build a team that works together, instead of against each other, and explains how to coach your employees to be valuable ambassadors of your company, instead of just another cog in the machine. By taking the necessary steps, you can turn a group of average employees into a team that blows away the competition.

THERE IS NO "I" IN "TEAM"

You hear this adage all of the time, but it is so true! If you want your team to function at its best, you need to encourage cooperation, *not* competition. The atmosphere at a company dictates much of the behavior of its employees. If your team is not functioning optimally, most likely there is something you can do to fix it. Patrick experienced this firsthand when his very talented, motivated, and organized executive assistant, Rita, came to him one day to give Patrick her two-weeks' notice. Patrick was upset, but assumed that she had received a better offer, so he asked her about it. He was startled to learn that Rita was making a lateral move to a similar company and was not getting a significant raise in pay or benefits. Patrick asked her, "Why are you leaving?" Eventually, she confessed to him that she was having an ongoing conflict with another employee on the team, Timothy. Armed with this information, Patrick implored her to let him mediate the issue and make an attempt to solve the problem before she left.

After several meetings between Patrick, Rita, and Timothy, the conflict was resolved. Rita was able to get a commitment from Timothy to stop barking orders and demanding that she drop all of her work whenever he needed help on his projects. Timothy also received a warning from Patrick that this type of arrogant and demeaning behavior would not be tolerated. The immediate result was that Patrick was able to solve the problem and keep two of his valued team members on board. More broadly, Patrick realized that he needed to (1) put more emphasis on cooperation among his team members and (2) provide an outlet to those who were having ongoing conflicts with one another. He also had to admit to himself that he had not been engaging with his employees as he should have been. Had Patrick been engaged, he would have been aware of the conflict and worked out a resolution long before Rita ever considered finding another job.

If you notice conflict among your team members, you have to address it head-on. You cannot simply ignore it and hope it will go away, because many times the best and brightest on a team will leave for greener pastures if their current environment is toxic. Even if there is no apparent conflict at the present time, you and your team can still benefit from going through the team-building exercises described in this chapter.

Whenever you have people working together, issues are bound to arise, but when you have already laid the foundation for how to work together as a team, these issues are much less likely to turn into full-fledged problems. The first step to resolving conflict is to gather your team together and ask some of the following questions:

- "What problems or challenges are we facing as a team?"
- "What opportunities should we take advantage of in the next few months?"
- "What is preventing us from working together effectively?"
- "What is our purpose as a team?"
- "Are we able to achieve that purpose right now?"
- "How can we be more effective?"
- "If you have a conflict with someone else on the team, how do you deal with it?"
- "Do you feel as if you can come to me to talk about a problem you are having with someone else on the team?"
- "How can I encourage you to perform better as a team?"

If you are aware of serious ongoing conflicts among your team members, you might need to have some one-on-one conversations before you hold a team meeting. Some team members may be unwilling to bring up their issues with others on the team, especially if this is the first time you have asked them to do so. In those cases, it may be best to meet with the troubled member prior to the team meeting, so you can get a full understanding of the conflict. Also, if there is a team member that you know is causing tension or strife, you should meet with that person beforehand and take steps to coach him or her to demonstrate the appropriate behaviors.

At this point, you might be starting to worry that you are going to end up spending all of your time solving your team members' problems. This is definitely not what we are advising. Once you have met with your team and established a consensus to operate as an effective team, you can turn much of the problem solving over to the members themselves. For example, one of the most frequent complaints a manager hears is, "I'm behind because I don't have the work I need from another team member." When managers hear this, they often get involved to rectify the situation. Of course, we would love it if our employees were able to address this situation on their own, but we cannot expect them to do this unless we give them the tools.

During your next team meeting, introduce this set of steps and questions that you want your team members to use when they have a problem with another member of the team.

Step 1—Janet needs data from Joe before she can write her report, but Joe has not given her the information she needs. Instead of approaching you, she asks Joe: *"Joe, I need this data by Friday. What can I do to help you get it done?"* Notice that this question is framed in a very positive way. It is not negative or accusatory, and it includes a sincere offer of help. Hopefully, Joe will communicate to Janet what he needs, and all will go well. If not, Janet should move on to Step 2.

Step 2—If nothing happens after Step 1, Janet needs to proceed by asking Joe: *"I need this work by Friday. Who else do we need to get involved in order to get this done?"* This question takes the

18

responsibility and puts it on the team as a unit. Janet is making it clear she will now get others involved to ensure that they are able to meet their deadline. Once again, we hope that this spurs Joe to action, but if not, the team will have to move on to step 3.

Step 3—Now the team is involved and putting peer pressure on Joe in order to get him to finish his work so they can meet their collective deadline. Janet now asks the team, *"We're trying to meet this deadline. What do we need to do to resolve this issue?"* At this point, the team must brainstorm and work together to solve the problem. We hope that Joe gets whatever help he needs and feels enough urgency to step up and get the job done. If not, the team finally moves on to step 4, at which time they involve the manager.

Step 4—Now that the team has exhausted all other options, they can legitimately go to the manager and say: *"Here is what we have done as a team. We are under a strict deadline; what should we do next so we can meet it?"*

As you see in this process, going to the manager is the last resort, not the first. The team does not wait until the deadline has been missed before bringing the problem to the attention of the manager. They can list all of the steps they have taken to resolve the problem and then find out from their manager how they should proceed.

This step-by-step process empowers your team to mediate problems *on their own*. How many people out there feel like there are others on their team who regularly slack off and do not do what they are supposed to do? This process gives those employees the tools they need to hold each other accountable. At the same time, no one on the team can give the excuse that they could not get something done because someone else did not do his or her job. It is everyone's responsibility to make sure that deadlines are met, and if one individual is holding up the process, then the rest of the team needs to step in and move the process along. Too often, egos pull teams apart and prevent them from working as effectively as possible. Team members frequently become too focused on their individual goals in order to receive accolades. In this way, they sacrifice the health of the team for individual success. As a manager, you can prevent this (or reverse it, if it has already happened) by creating unity among team members.

How do you create a unified team? You start by deciding on your team's purpose and goals. This should be a collaborative effort, involving all the members of the team; it should not be dictated by you, the manager. This does not mean that as a manager you have no say. It simply means that your team has to reach consensus on what they want to accomplish, otherwise there will be no buy-in, no sense of team ownership of the goals.

Once your team has decided on its purpose and goals, it is your job to strongly encourage that they work together. One of the ways to do this is to offer an incentive of some type—recognition, a commission, compensation, or awards for *team achievement,* not individual achievement. By doing this, you ensure that team members will do their best to help the team, rather than just themselves. The incentive or recognition does not have to be something that the company is not already doing; you might, however, need to tweak current reward programs so that they acknowledge the entire team rather than one or more individuals. For example, many companies award an "employee of the month," which could easily be changed to "team of the month" in order to encourage cooperation and teamwork. The members of the team will then hold each other accountable and, on the flipside, bend over backwards to help anyone on the team who needs it.

This concept can be difficult to implement at first because you have to resist our cultural norms that value individual success above everything else. For example, your company may harbor a very competitive environment, so you will have to change that if you want your team to become cohesive. Most of the time, however, it is easy to make this switch because you as a manager are responsible for the productivity of the 5, 10, or 100 people you manage. You are not evaluated on how each individual performs, but rather on the productivity of your entire team. This process requires you to pass down that type of thinking to your team members. Make your team accountable for the result; encourage team members to help one another out; and praise your team as a whole when they are victorious.

You may be wondering if this type of team building can work when your team does not work at the same site. The answer is yes. Even if you manage a team with some members working from home, or your team consists of individuals on three different continents, or you are a small (or large) business owner who manages independent contractors, you can still implement these principles of cooperation and noncompetitiveness. The key is to constantly circle back to the team when discussing projects.

Insist that conference calls be attended by all members of the team, and relate problems and solutions to the group, not one individual. Likewise, insist that members of the team communicate with one another, not just with you. As we discussed previously, assign deadlines, offer incentives, and institute penalties for the group, not just an individual. If conflicts arise, make sure the group addresses them, and resolves them to everyone's satisfaction.

MANAGING ATTITUDES AND ACTIONS

Sometimes it is not enough to change the actions of your team members; you have to manage their attitudes, as well. This may seem like an impossible task: How are you supposed to control someone else's attitude? But it actually is fairly simple. Managers create the "weather" in their own departments. If one manager greets her employees every day with a smile on her face and genuine interest in how they are doing, you can bet that they will feel good about coming to work each morning. Conversely, if another manager barks orders and fails to respond to friendly greetings, his employees will dread Mondays and act as if they want to be anywhere but the office. Employees respond so much better to positive communications instead of negative ones. As a manager, you have the power to make that happen. Take time every day to give some recognition and appreciation. Not once have we heard an employee say, "I wish my boss would stop being so appreciative of me!" Positive acknowledgment is something your team needs, and it does not cost you anything except a few seconds of your time. If everyone in the office seems down, find out why, then figure out what you can do to bring them back up.

Another simple way to manage attitudes and morale is to play to your team members' strengths. For example, if Bob is an incredibly shy person who literally gets sick to his stomach when he has to speak in front of others, do not constantly assign him the task of giving your team's presentations. Conversely, if Barbara loves to talk to new people and thrives on the energy of others, do not insist that she always be the one who stays behind while the rest of the team travels to conferences. These sound like no-brainers, but we have met too many managers who ignore their employees' strengths and weaknesses and then wonder why their workers are either miserable or not performing at their true potential.

At this point, you might be wondering, "How do I get tuned in to my team?" The first thing to do is to simply *listen* when your team members talk. Put away any phones, laptops, or other technological devices, and give your team members your full attention. Ask them individually how they are doing and what they like and do not like about their jobs. Do not be afraid to hear some complaints, and try to respond to any requests they have as quickly as possible. If your team members seem reluctant to open up to you about what is going on, you should also utilize these other tools at your disposal:

- Customer/client surveys
- Anonymous peer assessments of all members of your team
- Self-assessments by all members of your team
- Monitoring of team member activities:
  - Drop by during their presentations.
  - Carefully review their reports.
  - Keep track of whether or not they meet their deadlines.
  - Accompany them on client calls.
  - Generally, make time to see firsthand how they are doing their jobs.
  - Hold regular performance evaluation sessions for individuals and the team to let them know how they are doing, what is going well, and what needs to improve.

Ideally, if you do all of these things on a regular basis, your team will excel. They will learn that each person on the team is important and valuable, that they should work together, and to act graciously to one another and customers. When this is not the case, however, you will need to make changes to improve performance.

HOW TO MAKE A CHANGE

There are lots of different types of changes that a team faces, and just as many types of reactions to those changes. The executives in your company, for example, might decide to raise your team's monthly quota by 20 percent without soliciting any input from you or your staff. Or, one of your most productive team members might have to go on temporary medical leave, or even permanent disability. The company may start outsourcing jobs to another country; or you might have to hire someone who turns out not to be a good fit with the rest of your team. Change can even be something more benign, such as a new computer system or protocol that everyone now has to learn. Whatever the change, there is likely to be someone on your team who is unhappy about or resistant to it.

What is the best way to introduce change, and what should you do when the reaction to it is negative? We recently worked with a corporation that billed itself as "family-friendly," and its flexible-hours policy had attracted a lot of working mothers. As we began working with the company on team building, we learned about a serious backlash that had occurred over a new policy forbidding the use of personal cell phones in the office. Many of the employees complained that they needed to use their cell phones at work in case of a family emergency. The senior vice president, Cheryl, was being inundated with emails and phone calls protesting this policy, causing productivity at the office to hit an all-time low, because the cell phone ban was all anyone was talking about.

We started to address the issue by asking Cheryl how the policy had been announced. She told us that the company had sent out a memo, via email, on a Friday afternoon to all employees, notifying them that the cell phone ban would take effect Monday morning.

Upon hearing that, we gained good insight into the real issue. Understandably, there was anger and frustration among the employees because they were given no say in the decision-making process, and the change was announced abruptly on a Friday afternoon, leaving them plenty of time to stew over it throughout the weekend. Also, there was no time to ask questions or have a discussion about the policy change, because it was put into place almost immediately after it was announced.

We next asked Cheryl whether the company had predicted there would be resistance to this policy change. She replied, "Of course we knew; that is why we did it on a Friday afternoon. We thought everyone would get mad over the weekend and then be settled down by Monday. That is also why we chose to distribute the announcement via email; we did not want to have a public forum in which people could air their grievances."

Obviously, this company had gone about instituting this change the wrong way. Even though Cheryl showed us data that reinforced the company's position that employees were spending a significant amount of company time on personal calls, it did not matter in the end. The company had angered their employees unnecessarily, and now it was forced to do damage control.

The first step was to uncover the real issue: determine why people were so upset. After talking with employees, we learned that the company had a history of making announcements through email so that employees would not be able to offer any input. Many employees felt that the executives at the company had a dictatorial style of leadership and treated them as if they were children. They regarded the cell phone ban as just one more example of this poor treatment. In fairness, however, we also had some employees confide in us that there were those among them who made many personal phone calls throughout the day, but they felt that everyone was being punished for the sins of a few.

When we asked employees about the specifics of the cell phone ban itself, many of them expressed concern that their children or spouses would not be able to get in touch with them in case of an emergency. In response, we pointed out that all of them sat at desks equipped with phones and that if a family member needed to reach them it would be just as easy to call the office landline. Although many employees initially paid lip service to this fact, they quickly returned to their rants about how the company had treated them poorly.

After only a short time on site at this company, we quickly determined that the issue was not the cell phone ban, since the employees still had access to phones should a family emergency arise. Rather, the anger and discontent of the employees stemmed from the way this particular company had chosen to adopt policy changes. Once we had come to that conclusion, we shared the following insights with Cheryl and the other executives. We informed them that making frequent, unilateral decisions with no employee input was a recipe for disaster. Doing so disempowered their employees and made them resent any little change. Instead, we recommended they follow our guidelines for implementing change in order to garner employee buy-in and improve the currently hostile work environment.

Guidelines for Change

1. Avoid dictating rules to your employees whenever possible.

2. Ask employees to volunteer to serve on a committee that meets regularly with management to discuss concerns over current policies and proposed new policies.

3. When announcing a new policy, do it in person, if possible. Empower those at the middle and upper levels of management to discuss policy changes with lower-level employees.

4. Allow for a discussion period between the announcement of a new policy and its implementation. During this period of time, it is important to be willing to negotiate with your employees. Be prepared to be a little flexible on your policies, as this will show your employees that you value their input.

5. If employees have concerns about a policy, ask questions to discover whether those concerns are legitimate, or if the employees are simply afraid of change or are trying to avoid correcting bad behavior.

6. Be as honest as possible about the reasons behind proposed changes. If, say, you have data showing that the average employee spends two hours each day surfing the Internet for personal reasons, share that information with your employees before implementing a new online use policy.

7. If an employee repeatedly objects to policy changes, meet with him or her to discuss this resistance. It may be that this person is simply very vocal, or it could be this person does not want to do the job he or she was hired to do.

8. If you institute a change and it turns out to be a mistake, admit you were wrong and reverse the policy. Do not stubbornly cling to a rule just because you do not want to acknowledge you were mistaken.

In the end, the cell phone ban stayed in place. The company had good reasons to implement it, and it worked. Productivity increased as employees spent significantly less of their time on personal calls. However, the company also agreed to create committees to examine and discuss future changes, and those committees included employees from every level and department.

CONCLUSION

As a manager, you want to have all the answers; you do not want to look stupid—no one does. But you also have to empower your people to come up with their own answers. You cannot spend all your time solving everyone else's problems. The beauty, and value, of the questions in this chapter lies in the fact that you are allowing your team to solve their own problems whenever possible.

Team dynamics are complicated and something that many managers struggle to understand. If you follow the advice we have provided in this chapter, however, you should be able to demystify the process of building a winning team. In doing so, you will not only lead your employees to be much more effective and productive, but you will also reduce the amount of time you have to spend putting out fires that ignite between disgruntled team members.

CHAPTER 3

Questions That Delegate

What does it mean to delegate? So many people misunderstand this word and underestimate how complex the delegation process can be. Delegating is not about giving another person a job to do that you do not want. It is our belief that delegating is empowering others to grow, professionally or personally, while utilizing the company's resources effectively. Delegating also involves leveraging the talents and intelligence of those who work for you, while sharing the load and letting go of some of the day-to-day problems that you normally encounter. Finally, it is cultivating the gifts of those subordinate to you so that they are ready to take over your job when you get promoted.

For many managers, the advice to "let go" and delegate some of their responsibilities to their employees is a major challenge, one that is very difficult to meet, for often it represents a paradigm shift from their past behaviors. People in positions of authority generally get to the top by taking control and getting things done. The idea that they should now step back and let someone else take over areas of responsibility can be uncomfortable, frightening, and even feel a little dangerous—like an unnecessary risk. The problem is that many managers are already doing too much, and if they are successful in expanding their department or business, their responsibilities will only increase further. If a manager is unwilling or unable to delegate, inevitably problems will mount over time, and his or her success will necessarily be limited—one person can accomplish only so much.

On the flip side, delegating offers numerous benefits to you, as a manager. For one, it allows you to maximize your resources. Hopefully, you have hired talented individuals whose skills and intelligence strengthen your team. Delegating lets you tap into all that talent, to improve your department and, thus, your company. Furthermore, when you delegate, you encourage and empower your employees to grow and mature in their roles, which in turn makes you look good as a manager. With all these benefits, why do so many managers fail to delegate?

Here is an example of the type of client call we receive all the time: Alicia started her own business nine years ago. At first, she ran the business from a corner of her living room. Next she expanded it into her basement and then into her sister's house. Now she has a 10,000-square-foot warehouse and is charting revenues of $8 million a year. She is, by all measures, successful and living the American dream; but she is also exhausted, has no personal time, and has a family that is feeling shortchanged. And though the business is profitable, growth has leveled off during the last two years. Alicia knows that if she wants her business to grow further, she is going to have to learn to delegate significant responsibilities to others.

Sadly, fear is holding Alicia back, because she sees her workers either as incapable of taking on more, or not as hard-working as she wants them to be. So she turned to us for help. To an outsider, the problem is apparent. The skills and behaviors she expertly used to launch and build her business have led to trouble now that the business is large and successful. She can no longer come in early to work on special orders or personally visit all of her large-volume customers. Nor can she continue to be the only person who puts out fires in customer service and oversees the marketing team—not if she wants time to step back and focus on the big picture. She recognizes that if she does not change, she will either burn out or her company will continue to plateau. Plus, Alicia never forgets she has 90 employees whose livelihoods depend on her. If something happens to Alicia and she is unable to continue at this frantic pace, there is no succession plan—no one to take over the business and keep it going.

Alicia desperately needs to learn how to delegate and get others to step up. She has to stop sending the message to her employees that she will always be there to pick up the slack. Instead, she has to learn how to dole out responsibility, and then hold her employees accountable for doing their jobs and doing them well. She has to stop spending all of her time in operations putting out fires, so that she can have time for strategic planning. If she wants her company to grow, she needs to create and execute a plan for that growth. No longer can she attend just to the here and now; she has to learn to look toward the future, as well. Only then will she be able to grow her business, to focus on the direction she wants to go next, and to finally relax and take a little time off. More than anything, she needs to regroup. She has not taken a vacation for the last eight years, and Alicia is burned out.

Generally, there are four major reasons why managers do not take advantage of the fantastic opportunity that delegating presents. The first, as we mentioned in Alicia's case, is fear. They are concerned that they will give their employees something to do and that it will not be done correctly, or up to their expectations—the employee will not be able to complete the task as quickly or effectively as the manager. Because managers do not want to be seen as incompetent, they often worry that one of their employees will fail to deliver and cause a problem, which then will fall right back into the manager's lap, potentially raising concerns about his or her leadership abilities.

The second reason is control. Certain managers want to control as much as possible within their realm of responsibility. This type of leader does not want to relinquish any power, because he or she needs to be regarded as the person who "gets things done." For example, IT managers often relish being seen as the technology experts in the office. They like it that everyone comes to them to troubleshoot all the computer hardware, network, and telecommunications problems that arise. It is understandable that many IT managers start to thrive on feeling important, making it hard for them to let go and allow others to earn reputations as experts in their field. If someone else can do my job, they think, then why would they keep me around?

Managers whose thinking is governed by fear or a need to control are especially noticeable in a bad economy because there is so much angst about job security.

The third reason for failing to delegate is lack of awareness. Some managers simply do not know how to delegate, so they avoid it. Or they blithely assume it is not an issue; they wrongly believe that they have no reason to delegate. Oblivious, they allow work to pile up around them and then wonder why they are stretched so thin. These are the managers who do not want to "burden" their employees with extra work, so they take on everything themselves. Unfortunately, they are also the ones who complain (sometimes constantly) about an imbalance between their work life and home life. While this posture may seem noble at times, in the end what it does is deprive employees of the opportunity to learn new skills, while keeping managers from mentoring, coaching, and developing new business.

Finally, there are managers who do not delegate because they lack confidence in their employees. They question whether their team members have the desire and the skill level to grow and take on more responsibilities. This lack of confidence soon finds its way into the psyche of the employees, until they too believe that they cannot do more than the menial jobs to which they have been assigned.

No matter what the reason, managers who are not delegating are not taking full advantage of the resources around them.

We should also make clear before going any further that there is a difference between *delegating* and *dumping*. Delegating involves giving others responsibilities that will empower them to develop their skills and grow in their positions. Dumping, on the other hand, entails passing off busywork to someone else so you do not have to do it yourself. If the job is tedious and mundane, and the person being delegated to do it would not see it as a growth opportunity, then it is not something that should be delegated. For example, there are individuals whose job it is to copy, file, shred, and organize paperwork. If there is no one on the payroll who is specifically assigned these tasks, then your priority should be to hire someone for that purpose. Do not waste your time or the time of your most talented, highly skilled employees on tasks that a high school or college student could do.

One particularly negative result of failing to delegate is that it can create employee animosity. Managers send the message to employees that they cannot be trusted to take on new responsibilities. As a result, employees do not feel valued or important. Why bother to take the initiative, they think, if they will only be shot down by their bosses? Unknowingly, managers who do not delegate may come to be viewed as selfish, uncaring, and/or control freaks by their employees.

5 STEPS TO EFFECTIVE DELEGATING

To delegate effectively, take these five steps.

Step 1: Choose the Right Person

The first step in delegating effectively is to determine to whom you will assign the work. As a manager, you need to match up the strengths of each of your employees with the tasks that need to be done. Once you identify a responsibility that needs to be delegated, ask yourself these questions:

- Who has the capacity to do this job well?
- For which of my team members would this job be a step forward in his or her career?
- What skills are required for this job? Which of my team members has those skills?

For example, imagine that you are a business manager for a large medical practice. Your responsibilities have grown along with the number of doctors, nurse practitioners, nurses, secretaries, and patients in the practice. Assume now that you want someone to take over the scheduling for all of the employees. You would need to look for someone who is extremely organized, diplomatic (to make sure the scheduling is fair), and strong-willed (so that he or she will not be unduly influenced by employees wanting the plum schedules).

Take the time to give this assignment the careful consideration it deserves—do not pass it off to an employee merely because he or she seems to have time available for an additional task.

Step 2: Plan and Prepare

The second step is to plan how the transfer of power will proceed. Schedule time to sit down with your chosen employee and explain how this assignment is to be handled. This will require preplanning on your part to detail (preferably through written instructions) what the task entails, followed by your directions for carrying it out. This means that, initially, delegating is not going to save you time. But we assure you that investing a few hours now will pay off in the future.

As a result of successfully delegating, you will have developed employees who can accomplish complicated projects on their own. This will then alleviate some of the load you are currently bearing, and ultimately make your team stronger and more successful.

Consider these questions while you plan:

- What are my expectations for this job? How will it be measured?
- Is there a step-by-step process that needs to be followed?
- What is the scope of this responsibility? How much authority will this person have to complete this project?
- What resources will be available to use for this project?
- What guidelines and rules need to be followed?
- What is the time frame for this to be completed?
- How is this task going to be evaluated? What will be the measure of success?

- How do I create a follow-up system to make sure the job is being done correctly?
- What are the consequences if this person is not successful in this job?

We once had a client who wanted to delegate the planning for the grand opening of one of his franchises in an industry where image is very important. He asked one of his employees, someone who had been with the company for three years, to take the reins on the project. The manager provided a budget and a few other details as a guideline for his employee. The employee proceeded to spend a huge portion of the budget to hire a big-name band for the entertainment, leaving very little for food, alcohol, and other party necessities. As a result, the party was a flop and guests left suspecting that our client might be having financial difficulties.

Afterward, there was a lot of frustration on the part of both our client and his employee, so the question we raised was: who was to blame? If you delegate a task to someone but fail to provide sufficient guidelines or rules for how it should be carried out, you risk great deviation from your expectations. What our client should have done was provide a budget that included an approximate breakdown of how much his employee should spend for each category. He should also have given his employee guidelines about the major components of the party, to ensure that nothing would be overlooked. Finally, he should have followed up with his employee (as we suggest in steps 3 and 4) to ensure that the plans for the opening were to his satisfaction.

Step 3: Hold Delegation Meetings

Once you have set out—in writing—the expectations for the task to be delegated, it is time to meet with your chosen employee. During this meeting, go over *all* the information you have gathered about what he or she needs to do to complete this task. Mention any possible pitfalls or problems that are likely to occur—and don't forget to point out that the lines of communication will remain open between the two of you for the duration of the period to complete the task. You do not want an employee who is afraid to ask you a question or let you know if there is a problem. Many employees are hesitant to share their concerns, thinking it may raise doubts about their abilities. Your job is to *skillfully* uncover concerns by asking good questions about the path your employee plans to take. After instructing your employee to write a plan for how he or she intends to accomplish this project, set up a second meeting, at which time you will go over the plan together.

At the second meeting, review the plan created by your employee. Give him or her the opportunity to ask for clarifications and suggestions. Then make any changes you think are necessary. Make sure to specify the time frame you have allotted for this project. At the end of this meeting, set up as many follow-up meetings as you think may be needed to see this plan through to fruition. This may entail weekly conference calls or monthly face-to-face meetings. The frequency and type of meeting depends on your schedule, in conjunction with the intricacies of the project.

This step ensures that your chosen employee will take this process seriously. We worked with a bank that was looking for someone to manage its brand-new branch, scheduled to open in two months. The first person they picked to oversee the opening failed to follow through on this step. She was asked to put a plan into writing detailing how she would hire the appropriate personnel, secure advertising for the big event, and arrange security protocol for the branch. Although this first candidate did a good job verbalizing her ideas, she never completed the written plan. Therefore, the bank decided, wisely, to find someone else to take the helm of this project. The second delegate provided a 12-page detailed outline for how he would run the opening. He was tasked with the job because of his initiative, and he ended up succeeding beyond anyone's expectations.

Step 4: Follow Up

Follow-up is the most vital step in the process, while your employee is working on the assigned task and you check on the progress at regular intervals, make yourself available for questions, and assist if need be. This does not mean you should jump in and take over if a problem arises. Your role now should be more advisory. If you see your employee going astray, offer a suggestion for how he or she could do things differently. Ask questions to understand his or her reasons for making certain decisions; and if you don't agree with them, flesh out alternatives that might yield better results.

As long as you followed the first three steps, you should have an excellent plan in place for carrying out this project. Now let your employee follow through on this plan so that he or she can gain confidence and experience. Remember, your employee will develop this confidence by working through the problems that arise and the issues at hand. Confidence will not result from you stepping in and taking over.

During follow-up, it's a good idea to ask comparison questions to get at the heart of how the project is proceeding. For example, your first instinct might be to ask, "How is everything going?" Instead, ask, "In relation to the time frames we established, how has the project progressed this week as compared to last week?" Other comparison questions might include:

- "Can you walk me through some of the steps you have taken since our last conversation?"
- "How far along is the project today as compared to where you projected it would be when we first sat down to plan it?"
- "Which steps have been easier so far to implement than you planned?"
- "Which steps have been more difficult so far to implement than you planned?"

We hear from individuals on occasion who take ideas from our seminars and use them in their personal lives. Here is one interesting example we would like to share: A businessman for years had listened to his children beg to plan their annual family vacation. The kids accused their parents of being set in their ways, because they always wanted to go to the beach for a week in the summer. Finally, when the kids were 17 and 14, the father acquiesced. He gave them specific guidelines and a budget, and asked them to come up with a written plan for their upcoming vacation. The children decided they wanted the family to take a hiking trip along part of the Appalachian Trail. Our businessman friend was very resistant to the idea at first, as he imagined all of the things that could go wrong, but he nevertheless let the kids run with it.

It turned out to be the best vacation the family ever had. The kids had done their research and found some sites online that offered advice about how to prepare for the trip and sights to see along the way. On the third day, when the skies opened up and the rain started to pour, the kids just smiled and pulled out ponchos for the whole family to wear until the storm passed. Our friend decided then and there to let his kids plan all of the family vacations in the future. He had delegated this task to them, and by following up with written plans backed by thorough research, they had succeeded admirably!

Step 5: Evaluate, Offer Feedback, and Move Forward

Once your employee has completed the delegated task, it is time to conduct an evaluation. Sit down with your employee once the project is completed and ask him or her to self-assess how it went. Then you should provide a verbal and written performance assessment of your employee's performance. Include any suggestions that you think will help this person to perform better in the future; and be sure to give praise where it is due.

Remember, delegating is about developing talents, skills, and confidence. It is more important to focus on the positive aspects of an employee's performance, and the future, than it is to harp on minor mistakes. Once an employee has proved that he or she can handle a specific type of assignment, you can be confident in delegating other, similar work to him or her. On subsequent projects, however, you should still follow steps 2 through 5, but now you can give your employee more leeway to present creative alternatives to your suggestions.

WHEN DELEGATION DOESN'T WORK

If your first foray into delegation is not a success, look back over the steps to identify where the problem occurred. You might want to ask yourself the following questions to help get to the root of the issue:

- Was the delegate the wrong person for this job?
- Was the project too big for one person to handle?
- Did I provide sufficient guidelines for this assignment?
- Was the employee's written plan inadequate?
- Was I as available to help with problems as I should have been?
- Did I monitor his or her progress when I said I would?
- Were my expectations unrealistic?
- Did the employee follow through with the plan as it was written?
- Was the problem foreseeable?
- Does this employee deserve a second chance at this type of project?
- Did I make it easy for my employee to approach me?

If you do encounter a problem, make sure to discuss it openly and honestly with your employee. He or she deserves feedback, and you need suggestions on how better to handle delegation in the future. Sometimes employees are simply not ready to take on more important tasks, and in other instances, managers do not provide as much support as an employee needs to succeed. By asking yourself the questions above, you can determine which type of situation you are dealing with and then proceed from there.

WHEN DELEGATION WORKS

You may be starting to wonder if delegation is worth the effort. We want to assure you that it is. When it works, your employees will thrive, because they are using their skills and talents to their fullest potential. Instead of ducking work, they will begin to ask for more responsibilities because they know they are valued members of the team who can accomplish a great deal on their own. For you, successful delegation means a more effective and productive team. It also means you will have more time to develop your own skills and pursue projects that are of interest to you, because you will not be spending all of your time putting out fires or doing the work of others.

In closing this chapter, we want to give you a final example of how delegating can succeed beyond any expectations. Forty years ago, most primary care doctors worked in solo practices and did their own billing. They may have had one or two nurses working for them, but otherwise they did everything on their own, from seeing sick and well patients to calling in prescriptions to collecting payments to making sure that their offices did not run out of paper towels. Along the way, many of them realized that they could delegate certain responsibilities to others so they could focus on patient care, make more money, and expand their practices. They hired nurse practitioners and physician assistants to see patients with routine ailments. They tasked nurses with ordering medications and calling in prescriptions to pharmacies. Many hired business managers to oversee their staffs and run their billing departments, and secretaries to make their appointments and stock office supplies. Not only did these doctors grow their businesses, they were able to create jobs for others and find more time for themselves along the way. This is at the heart of why delegating is so valuable: It gives you time to plan for the future *and* enjoy the present.

CHAPTER 4

Questions That Coach

Have you ever found yourself thinking these thoughts?

> "I know I should coach my employees to develop their skills, but I just don't have the patience. Whenever I have tried to coach someone to improve their skill set, I end up biting my tongue so I don't shout, 'How many times have I told you how to do that? What is it going to take for this to sink in?' I don't want to blow up at my employees and say something I might regret later on. It's just easier if I do it myself."

Many managers feel this way, and thus let their perceived lack of patience limit the success of their team.

Coaching and delegating go hand in hand. The process of coaching stresses the importance of developing skills in your employees. When done well, it produces a stellar team by increasing overall success. There will be times you will need to coach an employee before you can delegate a particular job to him or her. At other times, you will need to coach in order to raise an employee up to a higher level of performance. When you coach, you *teach* skills; you do *not* lecture. It's an important distinction to make. To coach effectively, you need to allow sufficient time to carefully instruct an employee on how to excel at a particular skill. One of the best analogies for business coaching is coaching in the athletic arena.

A good basketball coach is not going to sit his team down and give an hour-long lecture about how *he* played the game. He is going to focus on the fundamental skills his players need in order to succeed. For example, he might first explain the correct form for shooting a foul shot, then quickly demonstrate how to do it, and, finally, have his team practice shooting foul shots for the next hour, while he stands by and gives suggestions. If they are unsuccessful, he is not going to grab the ball and say, "I'll just do it for you." He will explain what they are doing wrong and then patiently encourage them to practice again and again until they get it right.

Unfortunately, coaching, in the true sense of the word, is very rare in the business world. More commonly, you will find managers who have incredible skills but do not have the ability or the know-how to transfer those skills to their team. How many times have you met someone who excelled at his or her job, someone from whom you could learn a great deal, only to be disappointed that he or she could not, or would not, share those skills with you? For those of us who desire to be successful in the business world, this is the norm. We start out working for incredibly smart and talented individuals and hope to learn from them. Instead, we are disappointed to find they are either too busy to coach us; or, rather than coaching us, they simply do the job for us. They might think that we do not need coaching because we are already good at our jobs. Or, they believe that if we needed something from them we would ask. The result for those of us who want to be coached is that we probably are not performing at the highest possible level because we do not have someone available to assess our skills and help us make the necessary changes to improve. We still can learn a great deal just by watching highly skilled managers in action, but not nearly as much as if they were to spend time purposefully coaching us.

Regularly scheduled performance evaluations can be a starting point for managers to plan their coaching efforts. All too often, though, these review conversations are marked by generic phrases such as "take more initiative," "work smarter," "be a team player," or "needs improvement." When employees are evaluated in this cookie-cutter fashion, it is very difficult for them to make meaningful improvements because they are not given the specific steps they need to take. Instead, they are left to guess at what "take more initiative" might mean, and sometimes their guesses are way off.

For example, when Patrick was first starting out in his career, he worked as an expediter for the cylinder division of Parker Hannifin. He received two weeks of excellent training at the outset of the job. After six months of working at the company, he was given a performance review. His boss told him, "We really like you, and we think everything is going well. You just have a few things to work on at this time. You need to: (1) Develop better rapport with customers. (2) Improve your attitude. (3) Be more diplomatic in expediting. (4) Be on time for work." Now, to be fair, Patrick had been late twice in six months, so he at least had some clue as to where that directive was coming from, but the rest seemed to come out of the blue. He was given no coaching in the other three areas in which he was told he needed to improve and so had no clue as to how to address those issues. With the exception of #4, there was no way he could know how to implement change in ways that would lead to measurable results. How could he determine whether he was "developing better rapport with customers" or "improving his attitude"? What did that even mean?

The point is, coaching should be proactive and focused. If it happens during performance evaluations, that is fine. That said, it should not be limited to those meetings, because performance evaluations tend to focus on the past, whereas coaching has an eye on the future. Anytime you realize an employee lacks mastery of a necessary skill, you should schedule a coaching session. Then, when you meet with that person, you need to provide him or her with specific skills to work on, and give them specific directions for doing so—for example:

- Respond to customer service issues and/or inquiries within 24 hours.

- Create a mutual plan of action with the expediting division to fill rush orders.
- Schedule weekly meetings with your team to discuss problems, solutions, and successes.

Even managers who want to coach are often stymied by the prospect because it can be so difficult. When we consult with managers who need to coach their employees, we typically ask them to show us how they would go about coaching someone on a particular skill—frequently, on how to handle a disgruntled customer. Managers will usually get up in front of a room full of their employees and start talking about their experiences, what they have done well and how successful they are at dealing with angry customers. We often hear them use such phrases as "fix the problem," "make them happy," or "address the issue head-on." But then they fail to give their employees concrete ways to effectively fix the problem, make them happy, or address the issue. Thus, the employees leave these meetings with little actual understanding about how to go about solving very real problems; conversely, the managers believe they have "done their job" and inspired their employees to perform better.

Another good analogy to help explain coaching is parenting. Parents, of course, want their children to learn how to take care of themselves and skillfully navigate their world. However, many moms and dads get frustrated when their children are learning a new skill, because it seems to take so long. Rather than patiently coaching their children, they proceed to take over and do the task themselves. They clean their children's rooms, or tie their shoes, or do their school projects for them, instead of taking the time to teach their children how to do those things on their own. Needless to say, this does not help the child in the long run, because he or she does not learn these essential skills. Even worse, what the children *do* learn is to depend on others to take care of them. The same is true for our employees. If we do not take the time to coach them on the skills necessary to do their jobs, they will never learn them and will forever be dependent on us as managers to do their jobs for them.

WHY DO MANAGERS AVOID COACHING?

As you have probably realized by now, coaching takes a lot of time and patience. It is, in fact, much more time-consuming and labor-intensive to coach your employees on how to, say, give a business presentation, negotiate a contract, or rectify a problem on the production line than it is to do it yourself. That is why so many managers conclude they do not have the time to do this sort of hands-on teaching, and they do not see what the possible payoff would be in the future. Another factor is that the company culture may dictate that employees be given training only when they are first hired; thereafter, it is assumed that they know how to do everything their job entails.

A third reason managers avoid coaching is that doing it well requires a willingness to be vulnerable. In order to successfully coach an employee, you, as a manager, have to open up and share your thought process and the specific steps you take when completing a task. It can be very intimidating to reveal all of your "techniques," and to risk failure if they do not work. What you need to remember is that coaching is not about immediate results; it is about teaching the specific steps of a skill. Once that skill is mastered, success will inevitably follow.

Here's another good analogy: As part of their education, teachers go through a process known as "student teaching," during which they are paired up with a "master teacher" whose job it is to model effective teaching and classroom management techniques. The master teacher then watches as the student teacher practices these techniques in front of a classroom of students. This is usually a three- or four-month process, one that involves a lot of hands-on attention from the master teacher. If the student teacher makes a mistake or has difficulties disciplining unruly students, the master teacher is there to coach the student teacher on the steps to take to rectify the problem. Some experienced teachers volunteer on a regular basis to allow student teachers to come into their classrooms, because they have years of experience, skills, and knowledge they want to share. Other teachers avoid this experience because they do not want to put in the effort, or they fear a student teacher would not be success-ful and that the student's failure would reflect badly on them. Manag-ers have many of these same hang-ups and fears about coaching their employees.

A final reason managers may avoid coaching is because of the per-ceived risk involved. Many managers do not want to chance an employee jeopardizing business by botching an important project, so they limit how and when employees are allowed to practice their skills. This restricts an employee's development, however, because they do not get the opportunity to take the lead on difficult or im-portant cases. The solution is to assign simpler tasks at first and then raise the level of difficulty as employees progress.

Think about it this way: When you teach your teenager to drive, you start out in a parking lot, not on I-95 during rush hour. After some time, when your son or daughter has mastered the relatively easy skills needed for driving around an empty parking lot, you move on to neighborhood streets and then to more major roads. Eventually, you do let him or her drive on the highway during rush hour, but only after you have seen consistent success on slower, less-congested roads. This is the same process to use for employees. You do not want to give them the most difficult tasks first but you do not want them to stay in the parking lot forever, either.

STEPS TO SUCCESSFUL COACHING

Coaching cannot be done on the fly. It must be planned carefully and executed in a way that will allow for an employee to make mistakes, to get feedback, and to be given one-on-one instruction from a man-ager. That is why, to do it right, you need to ask yourself some ques-tions *before* you begin a coaching lesson.

- Why is it important that I coach?
- How will coaching benefit others? How will it help me?
- What are the consequences of not coaching?
- Who are the employees I need to coach?

- When am I going to start?
- What one skill am I going to focus on to help this employee strengthen his or her skills?
- How important is it for this employee to learn this skill?
- Given that level of importance, how much time each week can I devote to coaching this employee?
- What opportunities can I provide for this employee to practice this skill?
- What are the major aspects of this skill that the employee needs to learn?
- How will I measure these newly enhanced behaviors to ensure a successful outcome?

Once you have answered these questions, you can begin following the step-by-step coaching process outlined here—in this case, for submitting complete and timely reports.

Step 1: Explain your expectations—If one of your employees repeatedly submits late or incomplete reports, start your coaching session by explaining that you expect him or her to learn how to write complete reports and submit them on time. Outline the components of the report that are needed in order for it to be complete. Then show the employee a copy of a completed report so that he or she can see exactly what it should look like. Next, discuss how deadlines are set and what it means to meet them. This step may seem remedial, but we have seen more than one conflict arise because a manager wanted reports submitted at 9:00 AM on the morning they were due, whereas employees thought they had until 5:00 PM that day to finish them. Or, the employees assumed that submitting reports on time was not important.

Step 2: Get buy-in regarding the importance of this skill—Once you have explained your expectations, explain to the employee why this skill is so important. Continuing with the incomplete reports example, you might, for instance, detail for the employee the consequences of late and incomplete reports, such as the fact that colleagues are held up when reports are late, or clients become dissatisfied and complain when reports are incomplete. Help the employee to see the big picture—how his or her actions affect the company as a whole.

Step 3: Demonstrate the skill step by step and then instruct the employee to practice it—It does no good to discuss a problem with an employee if you never provide him or her with the specific steps to take in order to solve it. In this case, sit down with your employee and write a report together so he or she can see how you gather information, where to get the necessary data, and how to put it together properly. Then, give the employee a new report to complete and ask him or her to do it in front of you so you can be assured that all the steps are followed correctly. If your employee makes a mistake, quickly correct it and move on to the next step. Do not linger on criticism, or this process will become very painful—for both of you—and your employee will get discouraged. When your trainee does something well, offer quick praise and then continue with the coaching session.

At this point, it may be helpful to ask your employee a series of questions about this skill. It will illustrate why it is important, as well as help you determine whether more immediate coaching is required. Questions might include:

- "Why is this important for you to do well?"
- "Why is it important to the company that this report be done correctly and on time?"
- "When are you going to begin practicing?"
- "Are you willing to make a commitment to practice this skill? If so, when, how, and with whom?
- "Would it be helpful for us to practice together again?"
- "How are you going to measure your progress? Are you willing to do regular self-evaluations?"
- "Will you share with me the results of your self-evaluations?"

Step 4: Ask your employee to complete the task again, this time without your help—Once you have completed step 3 and are confident the employee is capable of successfully implementing this skill, ask him or her to demonstrate it again without your help. Give your employee another assignment, to complete a report by a given date and time. Make sure to allow plenty of time to complete the report, and check in on the progress halfway through that time period. Let your employee know that the lines of communication are open between the two of you, and that if there is a problem or question, you are available to help.

Once your employee completes the report, sit down together and go over it. Point out things that he or she did well, as well as those parts that still need improvement. Make sure you give plenty of praise, keeping in mind that one of the primary goals of coaching is to build confidence in your employees.

Step 5: Ask your employee for a commitment to continue working on this skill and give your commitment that you will follow up at set intervals—Coaching is not a one-time event, and in order for it to "stick" there needs to be follow-up on the part of both the manager and the employee. Once your employee has succeeded in completing a report to your satisfaction and on time, ask for his or her commitment to maintain this level of performance. Agree on a date and time when you will check in with one another to assess how he or she is performing; when you meet again, be prepared to give a written evaluation of the employee's performance of this skill. Likewise, instruct your employee to write a performance self-evaluation to share with you during this meeting.

WHEN COACHING IS NOT ENOUGH

If you have followed all of these steps and an employee still does not improve, what do you do? This is the most difficult part of being a manager. At this juncture, you need to either reassign the employee so that he or she does not have to complete the type of task at issue, or, if the task is a main component of the job, you need to let the employee go. This, of course, is a very upsetting step for most managers to take, but it does everyone a disservice to keep an employee on staff who cannot do the job. If this is the conclusion you draw about one of your employees, at least you can be confident that you tried your best to help this employee develop his or her skills.

Here are some questions to ask yourself when determining whether an employee needs more coaching, a different assignment, or to be let go:

- What was the employee's response to my attempts at coaching? Was he or she receptive or resistant?
- Did he or she follow up on the practice sessions we agreed to?
- Is this skill an important part of the employee's job?
- Is there another job he or she might be better suited for?
- Does he or she have the capacity to learn the skills needed for this job?

As we have all seen on TV shows like *American Idol*, a lot of people have the intense drive and desire necessary to accomplish great things, but, sadly, not all of them have the skills they need to do so. An employee might be likable, a hard worker, and a team player, all great qualities, but if he or she cannot do the job, none of that matters.

COACHING FOR THE FUTURE

Coaching requires an up-front investment of time and effort. The payoff comes in an increase in business and improvement in the quality of work your team accomplishes. Think about how much your team could achieve if each and every one of them had the skill set you do to excel in your business. This will help you realize that, at its heart, coaching is simply the process of passing down to your employees all the business knowledge and acquired skills that you have learned.

The number-one reason people cite for leaving a job is that they do not get along with their managers. If a manager does not coach, he or she risks losing the most talented and motivated people, because the best employees are those who want to be coached and develop their skills. Good employees do not want to wake up five years into a job and realize that they have not grown professionally from the day they started. If you fail to coach, you will, essentially, be encouraging your brightest employees to look elsewhere for opportunities and advancement.

For more information on topics discussed in this chapter, visit our website at: www.questionsthatgetresults.com/coaching.

CHAPTER 5

Questions That Motivate

When managers motivate, they inspire their employees to achieve truly breakthrough results. There are as many different ways to inspire employees as there are managers trying to inspire them! Some managers use contests, rewards, and/or bonuses to motivate their employees. Others use threats and punishments to keep their employees "in line." The one common theme that runs through all of business management, however, is that most managers do not ask their employees how best to motivate them. Instead, many managers end up playing a guessing game when it comes to deciding what will best motivate their employees—and, often, everyone winds up losing.

Here's a perfect example: Paul's client Rosa, the regional sales director for a Fortune 500 company, asked him, "Paul, what do you think about Jill's performance lately?" Jill was one of the firm's best salespeople; in fact, she'd recently celebrated her tenth year with the company. Paul told Rosa that whenever he had dealt with Jill, she struck him as a loyal, hardworking salesperson. Rosa agreed, but she was also concerned because the company had gone through a merger, as well as other complex changes, during Jill's tenure, and as a result it looked as if Jill was losing her competitive edge. Specifically, for the last three quarters, Jill's sales numbers had not been what they should be.

Rosa asked Paul, "What do you think we should do about Jill?" He responded to her question with one of his own: "Have you talked to Jill about this? Have you asked her how she feels about her performance?" Rosa nodded and said, "Sure. I've asked Jill plenty of times what's going on and how I can help her. She earnestly tells me everything's going well, and that she doesn't need any help. She keeps telling me that she has lots of irons in the fire and that I should be patient. But how long am I supposed to wait for her to get it together?"

Why had Rosa come to Paul about her problem with Jill? In our experience, most managers typically do not directly ask their employees about their motivation needs. They resist doing this for a number of reasons:

- They are afraid the employee might ask for additional resources that the organization cannot provide.
- They think everyone is motivated by money.
- They assume their employees are motivated by the same things that motivate them.
- They hope if they ignore the problem, it will just go away.
- They believe employees should motivate themselves.
- They wish to avoid the issue and any possible confrontation that might arise as a consequence of raising the question.
- They are afraid that, as managers, they might be part of the problem.
- They are so swamped themselves, they do not have enough time to spend with each employee.

What most managers do not recognize, though, is that the solution to any motivation problem lies in asking their employees the right questions!

There are numerous systems and explanations to describe how people are motivated, from Maslow's Hierarchy of Needs to Pavlov's dog. Experts do not necessarily agree on all the different ways people respond to incentives; however, as managers, we *can* learn how to recognize our employees' most common needs, ignite their drive, and then accelerate it.

From our experience in business and consulting, we have found that most employees want similar things from their bosses. Employees' "wants" generally fall into four categories:

- *Appreciation:* Who *doesn't* want to feel appreciated? Whether you are in a business relationship or a personal relationship, you want to feel like you and your needs matter. Employees want to feel valued by their employers. They want to know that they are important and that what they are doing has a purpose, a meaning. This goes beyond a paycheck and taps into your employees' emotional needs.

- *Guidance:* Employees want direction from their bosses. They want to clearly understand their responsibilities and goals. This gives employees a sense of security, because they are not treated as cogs in a machine—they know their employers value their contributions. To give good guidance, employers must provide measurable standards and expectations that are appropriate to each employee's particular position.

- *Communication:* An employee who is not kept in the loop is not a happy employee! Employees want to feel included in the decision-making process. They want to know what is going on in their companies and when changes will impact their positions. To communicate effectively, managers must "manage expectations" when they ask for employee input. This means that managers should ask an employee's opinion *and* make sure they let the employee know exactly how much weight that opinion will carry. Example: "I don't know what top management will ultimately decide, Josh, but how do *you* feel about this issue?"

- **Success:** Employees want to be on a winning team. They want to know that they are moving in a positive direction; and if they are not, they want to know what they can do to rectify the situation. No one wants to be a failure or a disappointment at work. Employees want to feel they are having a positive impact on the business. Obviously, all employees would like to take home the big bucks, but managers do not always have control over their compensation plans. That is why, as a manager, it is your responsibility to uncover other ways, beyond money, to make your employees feel successful.

Managers must recognize that all employees' needs in these four categories have to be fulfilled in order for employees to be motivated; at the same time, they must keep in mind that employees are individuals who differ as to *how* they want to be motivated. This is where the importance of questions comes into play. In order to determine how best to motivate your employees, you will have to ask each of them questions about themselves and their performance at work. This can easily become a standard component of your performance review system.

The following scenarios show how each of the four employee "wants" manifests. Following the stories, we have listed questions you can use to uncover your employees' motivational needs.

APPRECIATION

One of the most important things to remember about appreciation is that different people desire different types of appreciation. Here is a personal example: Recently, Paul had to travel extensively for business. He was in Washington, DC for a few days, then off to Dallas for a week, and then he had to go to New York for two nights. He returned home from this extended trip on a Friday night, around 9:30 PM. While Paul was away, his wife had assumed sole responsibility for taking care of their two young daughters, while working full-time herself. When he walked in the door, Paul was tired and stressed because he knew he would have to leave for yet another business trip on Monday morning; meanwhile, his wife was tired and stressed from doing double duty while he was away.

Paul just wanted to sit down and relax for a little while when he get home. His wife was clearly upset with him, but he did not know what to do. Paul asked her, "Honey, how can I help? What do you need me to do?" She answered, "Oh, Paul, I don't know! All I do know is I'm tired, overwhelmed, and frustrated that I have so much work to do. I know you need to travel for business, but it is really hard on me when you are not here. I just want to feel like I'm appreciated, that's all."

Here is another example: Dale, the son of one of Patrick's colleagues, started working as a high school teacher last year. While the family was together for the holidays, his father asked Dale how things were going with his new job. He replied that things were okay, but that he was not really enjoying his job very much. When his father asked him why, Dale told him that he just did not feel respected as a teacher. It seemed to him that the kids did not want to be there, and he was starting to wonder why he was putting in so much effort. Dale ended the conversation by proclaiming, "I feel like the kids don't really care, and it makes me not care, either."

One final example: One of our clients called us in after her company had conducted a sales competition between its sales associates. This seemed like a good idea to the managers because they thought it would inspire all of their employees to do their best. In reality, though, only one person could win the competition. Sure, the winning sales associate felt highly appreciated and satisfied with his win, but the *other* employees were left out in the cold. In fact, my client found that morale actually dropped dramatically following the end of this competition! Two of the firm's sales associates even tendered their resignations in the six months after the contest. When our client asked one of her top sales associates why he was leaving the company, he replied, "I'm disappointed with the way my year has gone, and I think it might be time to try something else."

In these three examples, Paul's wife, Dale, and the sales associate all wanted to be appreciated. It was not immediately clear what type of appreciation each of them desired, and most likely they did not all want the same form. The one thing they had in common was that they all wanted to feel valued and important; they wanted to feel like they mattered. As a manager, it is your job not only to dispense appreciation but to recognize that differences exist within your employee population. Some employees thrive on lavish, public praise, while others value private, understated commendations.

The best way to determine how an employee wants to be appreciated is to just *ask* him or her. This sounds easy, but it can be really difficult for some managers because they do not know the right questions to ask. Often, managers try to use simple praise to motivate their employees. Surprisingly, this can present a problem because praise can come across as insincere, or at the very least too general to be truly meaningful to an employee. How many times have you told someone "Great job!" or "Nice work out there"? To many employees those phrases are so generic and overused that they have virtually lost all meaning.

To jump-start the conversation, managers need to give specific praise and then follow it up with a question, such as the examples here:

- "You did a good job meeting the deadline on that project. How'd you manage to get it done so quickly?"
- "I like the strategy you used with that client. What made you decide to pursue that path?"
- "I think it's terrific that you've taken Kim under your wing. What have you found is the best way to teach new employees all that they need to learn?"
- "I admire the way you kept your cool in that meeting when everyone else was so agitated. How do you always stay so calm?"
- "Your presentation this morning was informative and entertaining. Where'd you learn to be such a great public speaker?"
- "Over the past three months, your organizational skills have kept the team moving in the right direction. Have you always felt comfortable as a leader?"

As you can see, these motivational questions are not scripts you have to follow. Rather, they are inquiries to get the conversation flowing so that you can show appreciation toward your employee; just as important, your employee has a chance to reveal to you his or her personality traits and professional needs.

What if you are faced with a situation in which an employee does not seem motivated at all? In order to get at the root of the problem, you still want to start out with sincere praise. You have to look for at least one characteristic you admire about this employee and then ask questions to uncover his or her motivational needs—even if that means spinning his or her negative traits into positives! For example:

- **To an employee who stews all day in his office:** "I like your intensity. Have you always been so intense when it comes to your work? What can I do to help your time here be less stressful?"

- **To an employee who has trouble meeting deadlines:** "I appreciate how much time and attention you give to the details in your reports. Unlike the reports I get from others, yours never have mistakes. What steps do you take to make sure your reports are flawless? How long does that process usually take? Do our usual deadlines give you enough time to prepare your reports? What can we do to help so that your reports arrive before the deadline, without losing your trademark accuracy?"

GUIDANCE

When employers provide goals and direction for their employees, then everyone is on the same page. Employees feel confident that they are spending time on projects that are vital to the company, and managers know their employees are on the right track. Without this type of guidance, employees may feel as if they are merely treading water, doing "busy work" while they struggle to read their bosses' minds. This lack of guidance can be very unsettling to an employee. Paul knows, because 10 years ago, it happened to him.

Paul was really excited to start a new job working for a man he respected very much; we will call him George Sparks. At that time,

Paul was working for another company and feeling very successful. Nevertheless, George wooed him away with promises of independence and opportunities. The hiring process took a significant amount of time, nearly three months. Paul was actually interviewed four different times by George and he was confident that someone who put so much thought into the hiring process would be a great boss.

He was wrong.

On his first day, George greeted Paul and they exchanged pleasantries for about five minutes. Then, just like that, he was out the door on a two-week business trip. As he left, he said to Paul, "The only way to learn this job is to do it." That was the extent of Paul's training! After all those months of interviewing and negotiating, he was in shock.

Paul really wanted this job to work out—after all he had a mortgage to pay and a family to feed—so he tried his best to do what he had been hired to do. For the first two weeks of Paul's tenure, George was away on business. During that time, Paul was left alone with only one coworker and no supervisor to turn to for advice. When George returned, things did not get much better. Paul would see him in passing in the hallways, but George never scheduled time to sit down with his new employee and find out how things were going or to ask what type of guidance Paul might need. With each passing day, Paul felt more lost and insecure. The only thing he *was* sure about was that, sooner or later, George would call Paul into his office and ream him out, telling Paul he was completely on the wrong track.

Paul eventually decided he could not take the uncertainty any longer. He contacted his previous boss and asked if he could have his old job back. His assurance that Paul was always welcome there was music to his ears. So Paul set up a meeting with George to give his notice. He was sure George would be relieved to hear he was leaving, because he knew in his gut this job was not working out. Much to Paul's surprise, when he told George he was going back to his former employer, George literally got tears in his eyes. Paul could not believe it. George told Paul he understood, and that he was sorry to see him go, but he never asked Paul why he was going or what he could do to convince him to stay. At the time, Paul was so anxious to get out of that office and that uncomfortable situation that he did not take the time to volunteer his reasons.

Who was ultimately at fault in this situation? The truth is, both George and Paul made mistakes. Paul should have asked more questions, to uncover the goals and objectives of his position. Likewise, George should have asked more questions of Paul, especially when he gave his resignation, so George could learn from his mistakes.

As managers, it is our responsibility to provide our employees with direction, and it is crucial that this direction be specific, focused, and measurable. Read through the directions given by two different managers here and judge for yourself which one meets those criteria:

Manager #1: "Okay, team, we need to get out there and pound the pavement. Our sales are down and we need to turn things around. This product isn't going to sell itself. We need to make new contacts, call on our old customers, and think outside the box. Be creative, and be persistent. All of our jobs are depending on these sales. Make it happen! Any questions?"

Manager #2: "Listen, team, we need to talk. As you all know, we have a new version of Product X debuting next month. We have 100 units of the old version sitting in our warehouses. In order to meet our quota for this quarter, we need to sell all 100 units of the older version before the new one comes out. As we all know, the older version of Product X is excellent, but the newer version has more bells and whistles. In order to encourage all of you to make quota, I'm going to increase your commission on Product X to 20 percent. Also, we're going to offer our customers a free extended warranty if they purchase the older version of Product X within the next month.

"I want you all to take a look at your existing customer base and think about those customers who might want to get in on this great deal. Focus on those who would prefer getting a good value over the newest version of a product. I also want you to explore prospective customers you haven't called on yet. Give them a chance to buy into this great value. Do you have any questions or concerns?"

In both cases, the managers are communicating with their salespeople that there is a problem that needs to be addressed. But the first manager left the salespeople on their own to figure out the solution. He provided very little guidance to his employees, which means he might be unpleasantly surprised down the road with the methods they use to address the problem. In contrast, the second manager gave specific, focused, and measurable direction to her employees. She ensured there would be no surprises, and that her employees knew exactly what she wanted from them.

It is simply not enough to tell someone on his or her first day on the job that he or she is expected to produce $500,000 worth of sales each quarter. That standard needs to be reinforced with clear-cut guidelines, to the point that the new employee realizes his or her job will be on the line if he or she misses the quota. The following questions will help you determine how much guidance your employees require and how much they already understand about what is expected of them. Of course, as a manager, it is important that you already know the answers you need to hear. However, you should also be prepared to hear answers that you might not have expected.

- "What are the three most important goals of your job?"
- "Describe for me what's expected of you here at X Company."
- "What does it mean to 'go the extra mile' in your position? Can you give me an example?"
- "What are the four major functions of your position? How should they be accomplished?"
- "What do you think separates a good employee from a great employee here at X Company?"
- "How do you know if you are doing a good job?"
- "If you had to explain your job to someone visiting from our corporate office, what would you say?"

- "Can you outline for me how you spend your week? How much time do you spend on each of the following: (1) making new contacts, (2) maintaining existing relationships, and (3) completing paperwork?"
- "What has surprised you most about this position?"

If your employees give you answers that do not match up with your expectations of their individual positions, then it is time to sit down with each of them and review the standards, goals, and objectives of their jobs. If your expectations are unrealistic, or if your employees' standards are too low, it is not necessarily anyone's fault. If this occurs, then you need to sit down and negotiate or clarify the standards for each position. This benefits the entire team in the long run. Your staff will be better employees and achieve greater success in their own areas, and you will not have to look for replacements.

COMMUNICATION

When employees do not get adequate, regular communication from their employers, they often feel unimportant and out of the loop.

Consider this scenario: You are the vice president of sales for a major corporation. You feel qualified and competent in your position, and you believe things are going really well. Then one Monday morning, the company's president calls an executive-level meeting. At the meeting, she unveils the company's new sales compensation program. It seems like an innovative and creative plan. The problem is, you had no idea that the company was looking at such a program in the first place! As the company's vice president of sales, how does this make you feel?

Here's another scenario to ponder: You work at a company that was recently bought out by a much larger organization. Everyone in your department knows that their jobs could be on the line. Each morning when you come to work, you hear another rumor about who will be laid off by the end of the day. Your department spends so much time speculating about the future that you are barely getting any work done. As the merger moves forward, no one from management offers you and your colleagues even an inkling of information about the future. How do you feel?

In each of these examples, you have been put into an uncomfortable situation because you are not receiving the communication you so desperately desire and need from your employer. This lack of communication may make you feel incompetent, unsure of your place in the company, and, worst of all, unimportant. This is something that many managers do not fully understand. The clients we meet with often have the attitude that they will provide information to their employees on *their* terms, on a "need-to-know basis." As you can imagine, this does not motivate employees; rather, it creates an environment where gossip, rumors, and festering resentment replace high morale.

Good communication, as we mentioned earlier, is essential to motivating your employees, improving their attitudes, ensuring they feel like part of the team, and making their jobs easier by giving them up-to-date information. Communication must go hand-in-hand with "managing expectations." This means that managers need to make it clear from the outset that they will consider employees' opinions, but that there are also many other factors that influence the outcome of any business situation, and that they must factor into the decision-making process. For example, a young friend of Patrick's family just started working for the local school district. When Patrick bumped into her this past summer at the grocery store, he asked her how things were going. She was frustrated, she said, because her principal had asked her and her fellow teachers to stay after school several days to come up with a new tutoring plan. The teachers had put a lot of thought and effort into the plan, only to have it scrapped before it even had a chance to be implemented. Understandably upset, she told Patrick, "I'll never volunteer to work on anything like that again."

The problem, Patrick realized, was that the principal had failed to manage the teachers' expectations. Instead of simply asking them to come up with a plan, she should have explained that though she wanted and valued their input, budget constraints might mean that the plan could not be put into place for several years. The outcome would have been the same, but the teachers would not have been so disappointed—or so angry at the principal.

As managers, it is often hard to know whether or not our communication style is effective. These next questions will help you evaluate your communication system and learn whether it's working and, if not, how to fix it:

- "What are some ways we can make sure everyone here is on the same page?"
- "Do you feel your ideas are given serious consideration?"
- "What is the best way to communicate with you on a daily/ weekly/monthly basis?"
- "Right now we send a daily e-mail to all our employees, along with a monthly newsletter. How effective do you feel those systems are at keeping you up to date on company news?"
- "Do you feel you have all the information/resources you need to be effective in your position?"
- "Who do you contact if you have an innovation you want to propose?"
- "I would like to get your input; what do you think of this idea?"

As managers, we all tend to acknowledge the importance of communication—superficially. We do not always act as if we truly believe it, though, until we see for ourselves the effects of bad communication. Last year, we worked with two companies with vastly different communication styles and saw firsthand how vital communication is to a company's success. We will call the companies Telco and Sky Tech.

Telco looked like it was going to have a great year. It had just landed a huge national client, in a deal worth $6 million per year, spreading revenue throughout their company's offices. Telco set sales quotas for each of its regional offices. Due to this great new deal, all of the regional offices were on the books as above quota, though the regional sales managers had not been part of the negotiations. The executives at Telco saw this as a problem: They did not want to give the requisite bonuses to their regional sales managers because, in reality, this was a windfall and the regional sales staff had not been part of the sale. Without consulting their salespeople, Telco's executives decided to raise the company's regional sales quotas in the middle of the fiscal year. They sent out a memo to that effect on Friday afternoon of the Memorial Day weekend. The execs thought—or at least hoped—the sales managers would be over their anger and irritation about this by Tuesday, when they came back from the long holiday weekend.

Meanwhile, Sky Tech was in trouble. It had just lost its biggest client and was looking at a losing year. The president of the firm called us to ask our advice. We suggested that he call a meeting of all of his regional sales managers to let them in on the problem and then ask for their advice. We knew he had some sharp minds on his staff, and we were sure they could come up with a workable plan for hitting these new targets.

At the end of the year, which company do you think was hitting its sales targets? Not Telco, even though it had landed a $6 million client. Following that Friday afternoon memo, Telco executives were faced with a swarm of irate sales managers. Company morale had sunk to an all-time low, and despite the new budget, sales were off for the next three quarters. Several of Telco's regional managers lost momentum and/or left the company, and those who remained felt betrayed.

Meanwhile, Sky Tech ended up having a good year; and the next year was its best ever. Its sales managers rallied behind the company, brainstormed innovative sales campaigns, and brought the company back from the verge of disaster.

One major factor in these opposing outcomes was clear to me. One company valued communication; the other did not. One company included the team in its communications; the other did not. The result: One company triumphed; the other failed.

SUCCESS

For employees to feel triumphant in their jobs, they also need to be respected. We want to share with you a trend that we believe is killing motivation in today's workplace. We have seen our clients use this strategy, and it almost always backfires.

In business today, none of us could function without the Internet and all of its accompanying resources. Every business professional we know depends more and more on its availability. About two years ago, clients began approaching us to ask our opinion about restricting their employees' Internet access at work. Our clients contend that their employees are wasting time at websites that are not work-related, thereby slowing down productivity. Whenever this issue comes up, we remind our clients that, today, their access to their employees is unprecedented, and vice versa. Employees are expected to answer e-mail from home, call in while on vacation, and generally stay tethered to the office 24/7. We point out to our clients that productivity has increased greatly over the past several decades, and they owe much of that rise to technology *and* to their employees who use it to stay connected to work.

Unfortunately, some of our clients stubbornly refuse to recognize the truth of this. They insist on installing programs to monitor and restrict their employees' Internet access. When this happens, employees are inevitably *not* happy campers—not because employees want to squander their work time with online shopping or Internet gambling—but because they feel they are being treated disrespectfully—like naughty children instead of the capable professionals they are. Employers must remember that they will reap what they sow and that nothing will make an employee's blossoming sense of success wilt faster than an employer who poisons the workplace atmosphere with suspicion and disdain. That is no way to motivate employees to go above and beyond.

The majority of employees come to work intending to do their best. If a manager notices someone is not performing well, he or she should address the issue as soon as possible, rather than ignore it until it snowballs into a major problem. You risk losing your best employees if you do not discover ways for them to be successful in their positions and accomplish their goals. The point is: An employee's feelings of success, or lack thereof, will spur him or her to work harder or drag that person into the doldrums. By having conversations with your employees about how they experience success, you can implement more effective programs, reward systems, and promotions, which will both satisfy your employees and encourage their productivity.

Here are some questions to draw out information from your employees about how they experience success:

- "What do you feel is going well for you at our company?"
- "What have you accomplished so far that you are really proud of?"
- "You're obviously very successful. Besides the obvious—a bigger paycheck—what else would make you feel more successful on the job? In life?"
- "How do you define success?"
- "Imagine it is five years from now. What would you have to accomplish in order to feel successful at that point in your career?"
- "What do you enjoy most about this job? What would you like to do more of in your position?"
- "What two things would you most like to achieve in the next six months?"
- "In this job, are you able to do what you're really good at?"

• • •

Next, we have included transcripts of two conversations in which managers ask their employees motivation questions. Someone who needs a little clarification or a pat on the back will most likely clue you in to those needs with his or her answers to your opening questions. These are the easiest types of employees to motivate because they are already willing to work hard—they just need some encouragement. Here is an example of that type of employee:

Manager: Jim, thanks for coming in to see me today.

Jim: Thanks for taking the time to see me.

Manager: I just wanted to check in with you to see how you're doing. I know you've been working here for three months now, so I wanted to touch base and see how things are going. Can you tell me what's going well for you?

Jim: I think there's a lot going well for me. I've opened four new accounts, generated some good revenue, and made great contacts.

Manager: You've certainly gotten off to a terrific start, and we're pleased with your results. Let me ask you another question: What about this position has surprised you?

Jim: Let's see . . . I've been surprised at how well I've gotten along with everyone here. It's been very easy to fit in with the other salespeople. (Jim's response here was superficial, so the manager needs to ask the question again in order to get a more concrete response.)

Manager: I'm glad you feel welcome here, as we pride ourselves on teamwork. It's vitally important for anyone starting a new position to feel welcome. What has surprised you about what's available to you in terms of your job's resources?

Jim: I must admit I was surprised that I didn't get more coaching. I was disappointed that I wasn't assigned a mentor. In some of these areas, I don't know who to turn to when I have an issue.

Manager: Do you have any questions about your position in the company?

Jim: Well, I do have a question about how many accounts I should be opening each quarter.

Manager: That's a great question. For your position, the goal should be three to five new accounts each quarter, with the average account worth about $25,000. That said, even though we set these goals, we are really more concerned about quality than quantity. We don't want you to open accounts that are not profitable. We would rather you open only two accounts with a 12 percent profit margin each quarter than to open five or six accounts where the profit margins are slim—or worse, the accounts actually *cost* us money. Also, we want you to spend time on maintaining current accounts. Our company prides itself on customer service, and we wouldn't want to neglect our longtime customers who have been the foundation of our business just to open unprofitable accounts. Does that help you?

Jim: Yes, that makes a lot of sense. I'm glad you could give me that type of clarity, so I can stay focused. I wasn't sure whether or not I should really hustle to open new accounts or focus on existing ones.

Jim's case is an easy one because he wants to be motivated, and he is eager to work hard. The only thing he needed was some guidance. He just needed to know in which direction he should be moving. After this meeting with his manager, Jim will most likely be reenergized and strive to continue to do his best on the job.

Other employees, however, will need a little more to motivate them. In these situations you will have to delve deeper with your questions. Next is an example of an employee who needs to be motivated. In this case, the employee has lost the spark she once had for her work. She has been in the same position for six years, and her production has become sluggish. Her manager did the research and discovered that her productivity had been down an average of 17 percent in the last 18 months. This manager has to figure out what has gone wrong and what he can do to jump-start this employee's motivation.

Manager: Meghan, thanks for coming in to see me today. I wanted to ask you a few questions about how things are going in your department. Tell me, how have your accounts been doing over the past year?

Meghan: Oh, they've been okay. Things have been a little slow lately. But I feel confident that my numbers will improve within the next few months.

Manager: I see. I'm sure things will improve, too. Why do you think the numbers have been low?

Meghan: Well, I just think that the market has been battering us around lately. Everyone has been feeling the pain.

Manager: I agree; things have been tough lately because of the market. The important thing is to focus on how we can improve these low numbers. What do you think we can do?

Meghan: Well, I don't really know what can be done. I've been doing the same things I've always done, but the clients seem so risk-averse right now.

Manager: Maybe there's something to that. We really appreciate your experience and the time you've spent with the company. You've done some great work, but perhaps it's time to rethink some of your methods. If you've been doing the same thing for six years, you might need to adjust your approach. It could be that you're bored, because you're not being challenged. Could there be any truth to what I am saying?

Meghan: (Responds after 10 seconds of deliberating) Yes, I think you're right. Lately, I've felt as though I haven't really been challenged as much as I have been in the past.

For the next 20 minutes, Meghan and the manager discuss how she has been bored and stagnating in her position. The manager does not want to write Meghan off as a lost cause, as she's been a successful employee in the past and her experience with the company is a valuable asset. As Meghan and the manager talk more, it becomes clear that she wants to get into more of a leadership role. For his part, the manager is stretched thin, and he could use some help in that area. He knows he has problems with retention and could benefit from help from someone with Meghan's experience. Meghan and the manager realize that perhaps a sales position is no longer right for her. Instead, she might move toward leadership and mentoring. (In fact, maybe she could even be a mentor to Jim from the previous example!) This could be an exciting new challenge for Meghan and at the same time, alleviate some of the stress on Human Resources.

At this point, Meghan and her manager continue their conversation.

Manager: If you're really up for a new challenge, Meghan, I have an idea. I know you've informally trained many employees in the past. Would you be interested in being part of a team that creates a formal training program? Human Resources has informed me that they're creating an orientation program for training new employees. It'll involve introducing new employees to our company policies, orienting them to company culture, and explaining our practices.

Meghan: I think that would be really exciting! There is so much that new employees need to learn when they first get here. It's hard for them because they're coming into an unfamiliar environment. I know it really helps to give them some tips and useful information. I'd like to test my abilities to manage and guide others. I've been successful here, and I'd like to continue here in some capacity.

In this second example, the manager asked specific questions to target the problems Meghan was experiencing. He recognized that Meghan was a good employee but that she was also no longer effective in her current position. Rather than trying to force her to "step up to the plate," this creative manager decided to involve Meghan in a different way. He guessed (correctly) that she wanted something new to challenge her, and he found a useful way to focus Meghan's considerable experience.

When managers motivate effectively, they inspire their employees to do their best. Employees who are motivated have a drive to succeed and are willing to do the hard work necessary to accomplish their goals. If motivating employees is such a big part of managers' jobs, you would think they would spend a great deal of their time working on motivation. But you'd be wrong. We cannot begin to count the number of times clients have called to ask for our help in motivating their employees. Usually, they do not even realize that the problem is a lack of motivation; they often conclude that they just have "lazy employees." Over and over again, clients have told us that their business would improve if only someone would "step up to the plate" or "put in that extra effort." Most managers do not think it is their job to inspire excellence from their employees. Others make the mistake of assuming that all their employees will respond to the same type of reward system. But, of course, employees are individuals, whose motivations are as different as their personalities and work styles; therefore, managers need to respond to those differences if they want their employees to perform above and beyond expectations. When employees are inspired to do their best, the sky is the limit!

CHAPTER 6

Questions That Hire

Just the thought of hiring a new employee makes many managers shudder! Sifting through endless resumes, fielding phone calls to make appointments, and then sitting through interview after interview takes its toll on even the most dedicated among us. Many managers dread having to spend even one more minute on the hiring process.

Does that sound like you? If so, I have good news and bad news. The bad news: There is no quick, easy process to follow if you want to hire the right person. The good news: By using the techniques described in this chapter, you will learn how to hire employees who will be amazing assets to your company, those who will not just "fill positions" but who will benefit your company now and in the future.

In 2004, a well-known financial services company hired Phil Fenton* as its sales director. During Fenton's nine months on the job, the company paid him $90,000. But in 2005, his employers fired

---

* This name has been changed for privacy purposes.

him because he had not done his job; specifically, they claimed he spent most of his time at work making personal phone calls or listening to music. Following his termination, Fenton's employers went a step further: The financial services company sued him for $300,000—$90,000 for his salary plus $210,000 in lost revenue. The company realized, after the fact, how vital the position of sales director could be. Its lawyers calculated just how costly it had been to employ someone who did not perform his duties well, and that total came to three times the salary of the position!

Think now for a moment about a position you need to fill, and ask yourself: Can you afford to lose three times the salary of that position by hiring someone who is not a good fit for the job?

At the present time, Fenton's case still has not been settled, and many believe it is unlikely that the company will ever recoup any of the money it lost during his brief tenure as its sales director. More to the point, it seems as though this company has not learned its lesson. Rather than bemoaning Fenton's poor performance, the company would be better off reviewing its hiring process—and perhaps firing whoever hired Phil Fenton in the first place. This company may not have learned from its mistakes, but you can.

When you interview to fill a professional position, you are wrestling with a decision that could either earn or cost your company hundreds of thousands of dollars. When you think in terms of those numbers, you realize just how important the hiring process is to a company's success and how ill-prepared many of us are to undertake this journey. This chapter will give you the tools you need to approach your next round of interviews with confidence, even enthusiasm.

Let the games begin!

• • •

Imagine this scene: You arrive at work on a stormy Monday morning. Even before you shake off your wet raincoat, you know you'll find piles of papers on your desk, and that each memo, fax, and letter needs your attention ASAP. In addition, email is overflowing your inbox, and you have eight voicemail messages you need to return, pronto! Then, just as you are ready to start your day, one of your best employees comes into your office to break the bad news: She must resign from her job to take care of her elderly parents. Now, in addition to everything else on your plate, you have to hire someone to replace her, and the sooner the better. You have a real crisis on your hands!

Your first step is to contact your Human Resources department to inform them of the situation. They ask you to give them some specific requirements to include in the want ad: What exactly are you looking for in a replacement? You sit at your desk and think. How do you even begin to craft a "want ad" for the person who can fill this important position? What qualities, experiences, and education should you expect your new hire to possess? What information should you learn about potential candidates in order to determine if one of them will be a good fit for your organization?

Exercise

Take a moment to consider how you would create an ad for a pivotal position in your company. Write it on the lines provided:

_____

_____

_____

_____

_____

_____

_____

Here are three examples of typical want ads we have come across recently:

Established company that just relocated has an outside sales position covering the mid-Atlantic territory. Ideal candidate will have experience in equipment sales in the medical field. Candidate must have previous equipment sales and service experience with hospitals, including nursing manager and staff. Experience selling to IT and pharmacy administrators a plus. Candidate must have a BA or BS degree, be high-energy, enjoy interacting with people, and be able to build lasting relationships with clients. Candidate will be required to submit weekly call reports, and must be a quick learner and self-starter.

• • •

Sales Director/Outside Sales Professional needed for a prominent, nationwide staffing firm. The successful candidate will:

- Have a minimum of two years outside, business-to-business sales experience, preferably in a service industry.
- Have perseverance and be sales-driven.
- Have a sense of urgency and a sense of commitment, with strong, follow-up skills.
- Have the ability and desire to "make things happen."
- Maintain a proven track record to meet targets, combined with high standards and a desire to be continuously challenged.
- Demonstrate time management, scheduling, and organizational skills.
- Have strong written and oral communication skills.
- Be a highly motivated, energetic, and quality-oriented individual.
- Have a dynamic, high-energy personality, and be a leader who is hands-on, and leads by example.

• • •

We have an immediate opening for an individual to help grow our business in this area. If you are high-energy, competitive, have a track record of sales success, and want to build relationships and control your income potential, please email your resume to us as soon as possible. Competitive salary, plus commission is provided. Excellent growth potential is available for the ideal candidate. Requirements: One year-plus experience in sales (outside sales is a plus); excellent people skills; a team player; history of meeting and surpassing goals; self-starter who can work independently to get results.

Like the ads of these managers, your advertisement would also have included experience requirements, a certain level of education, and keywords such as "team player," "flexible," "innovative," "hard-working," and "self-starter." These keywords are problematic, however, because they are impossible to quantify. If you cannot measure such qualities, how can you expect to determine accurately whether someone will make a good employee?

MEASURABLE VERSUS NONMEASURABLE QUALITIES

Take a look at the following questions and think about whether or not you would use them in an interview with job candidates:

- "Would you call yourself an innovative person?"
- "How do you think outside the box?"
- "In what ways are you creative in your current job?"
- "How are you motivated at work?"
- "Would others consider you to be self-motivated?"
- "How flexible are you in your work schedule?"
- "Are you willing to work on the weekends?"
- "Would you say you are good at multitasking?"
- "How well do you work on teams?"
- "Do you get along well with others at your current job?"
- "What do you like about being on a team?"
- "Do you take initiative at work?"
- "Are you able to work independently?"

What do you think about these questions? Many managers would admit that they ask this type of questions in their interviews and that the qualities they describe are important. The problem with them, however, is that they all focus on characteristics that are *nonmeasurable*.

Now read through this example of how this sort of exchange might play out during an interview:

Interviewer: Scott, I am glad you are here today. I want to ask you a few questions about working on a team. As you know, this position would require working with several other people in our Research & Development department. How well do you work with others?

Scott: I work great on a team! I love working with other people.

Interviewer: That's good to hear. Now, what about motivation? Tell me how motivated you are to get things accomplished at work.

Scott: I am really a self-motivated person who gets things accomplished. In fact, at my current job, I am the first person there in the morning and often I am one of the last to leave at night. I'm passionate about getting my work done.

Interviewer: Well, that's good to hear, as well. What about flexibility in your work schedule? You know, sometimes we have to work overtime here, and occasionally we need to work on the weekends, too. How do you feel about that?

Scott: That would be fine. I will do whatever it takes to get the job done.

Scott sounds like a manager's dream come true, doesn't he? He has defined himself as a team player, self-motivated, and flexible. These are the qualities that all of those want ads say they are looking for in a new employee—what's not to like? Just this: These are the kind of qualities that cannot be measured. Let's face it, most people interviewing for a job would describe themselves as team players, self-motivated, and flexible. That is why, as a manager, you must dig deeper to uncover *measurable* qualifications of potential employees. With that in mind, let's review some of Scott's answers to the typical questions managers ask.

The interviewer asked Scott if he was self-motivated, and Scott assured him he was. Scott went on to say that at his current job he is the first person there in the morning and often the last to leave at night. This type of answer impresses many employers. They would assume Scott puts in all that time at work because he is dedicated and determined.

That may be true. Or it may not be. Maybe Scott has a tough time with the technical aspects of his job, so he has to spend more time than his coworkers to finish a project. Or perhaps he's a highly social type, who spends more time chatting up his colleagues during the day than doing his work. Or Scott and his wife might have a rocky relationship, so he spends as many waking hours as possible at the office to avoid confrontations at home. Uncovering the real reasons behind Scott putting in so much extra time at work will help a manager to decide whether Scott would, in fact, be a stellar employee, whereas asking questions that focus on nonmeasurable qualities might lead the manager to draw the wrong conclusion.

A potential employee's measurable qualities vary according to the position for which he or she is interviewing. For a sales position, for example, measurable qualities would include the percentage of growth in sales figures for a 12-month period, the number of cold calls resulting in sales for a 30-day period, and the number of new contracts signed in a quarter. For a Research and Development position, measurable qualities would include the number of proposals that become prototypes within a 12-month period, the percentage of prototypes chosen for mass production each quarter, and the amount of money earned each year through the writing of grants.

As you look back at the example of Scott, you can see that the interviewer should have asked questions focusing on measurable qualities, rather than the nonmeasurable ones. Had the manager done so, here's what he or she might have learned:

Interviewer: Scott, you told me that you're very self-motivated. You said that you're the first person at work every morning and the last person to leave. I was wondering, how much grant money did you earn in the past year?

Scott: I was awarded $2 million in grants last year to work on product development.

Interviewer: That's great! How many grant proposals did you have to write in order to get that award?

Scott: Well, last year I only wrote three grant proposals.

Interviewer: Was the $2 million for three different grants?

Scott: Actually, it was for one of the grants I wrote.

Interviewer: Okay, how did you come up with the idea for that grant?

Scott: It was actually a grant that one of my colleagues had written several years ago. It was up for renewal last year and I submitted the renewal package.

Interviewer: I see. What other projects are you working on right now?

Scott: Well, I have several ideas for grants that I've been kicking around.

Interviewer: Do you have any other research going on at this time?

Scott: Not exactly. This $2 million project takes up a lot of my time.

Interviewer: It must be a pretty big project. Which part of it takes up the most time?

Scott: A lot of the research requires using equipment I've never worked with before, so it takes some time to get all of the procedures down pat.

Interviewer: I see. So is that why you've been spending so much time at work?

Scott: Yes, I guess so.

Now Scott does not seem like such a promising job candidate, does he? In reading this, you might be thinking, this is too easy. And it's true, we have made the scenario simple, to prove a point. However, there is an important lesson to take away from this example: Interviews are often made up of questions that garner few details about potential employees and leave too much room for them to charm managers by saying all the right things. Instead of coming away from an interview with just a "sense" of whether or not a candidate would be a good fit for the position, a manager should take away *concrete information* from the interaction. In this way, the hiring process will be based on *evidence* of candidates' past performances, not how well they got along with the interviewer. Asking questions about measurable qualities garners significantly more useful information than questions about nonmeasurable qualities.

Asking questions about nonmeasurable qualities is not the only mistake managers make when it comes to interviewing potential employees. Many also believe they can trust their instincts about people, that they can rely on their "gut" rather than finding more substantive reasons to make their hiring choices.

INSTINCTUAL INTERVIEWING

Like many managers, you might believe that once a potential employee walks in the door you will know "in your gut" if he or she is right for the job. Unfortunately, for a number of reasons, "going with your gut" often leads to a dead end when it comes to hiring. One important point to keep in mind is that, whether we mean to or not, we tend to hire people who are like us.

A politician we know loves to tell this story. His chief of staff was an effective and efficient leader, but she was a perfectionist. As the chief of staff, she was in charge of filling important positions in his administration. After a few years, he noticed that all the people who worked for him were also perfectionists—in short, the chief of staff was hiring people just like herself. While our politician friend applauded his employees' work ethic, he could not help noticing that projects seemed to take longer than he thought they should. In fact, he was irritated that his employees seemed to be constantly reworking projects, "fixing" details over and over again. One day, he called his chief of staff into his office because he had noticed some vacancies in the administration. He told her that while he appreciated the talent of all the people in his administration, he thought this would be an excellent opportunity to add some different personality types to the mix, to balance things out (and, he hoped, to see projects completed on time for a change!).

As the hiring process went forward, the politician took the time to sit in on some interviews. He made sure to ask the candidates questions such as: "If a project deadline was this morning at 9:00 AM and you noticed an insignificant typo in the document at 8:55 AM, would you let it go to make the deadline, or fix the error and turn the project in late?" He made sure to hire candidates who said they would turn the project in on time. This enabled him to balance out his staff of perfectionists, who excelled at focusing on the details but often had trouble keeping the big picture in mind.

This story is a perfect example of how managers, often unconsciously, hire people like themselves. Employers who graduated from Ivy League colleges tend to hire others who graduated from Ivy League colleges; mild-mannered managers tend to hire mild-mannered employees; and so on. If you are prone to this, be aware that it can lead to a situation where your staff has very little variety. A company staffed by too many individuals with similar personalities can stagnate over time and, ultimately, fail because of a lack of innovation. This can cost you money, as well. If new ideas or technologies are being implemented elsewhere, yet your company is playing it safe, maintaining the status quo, you will end up losing out on new opportunities. A company whose employees have a variety of different personalities, experiences, and beliefs is more likely to grow as employees collaborate, learn from one another, and join forces to brainstorm new ideas.

Another reason why going with your gut does not pay off in the long run has to do with the previous section. If you hire on instinct, you tend to focus on personality and nonmeasurable qualities, rather than on measurable ones. Instinctual hiring caused quite a headache for a client of ours. John is the vice president of an electronics company that sells and services equipment throughout the United States. About a year ago, he needed to hire a new manager for the southwest division, someone who would coordinate and evaluate the work of 20 employees, develop new contacts, and write quarterly reports. He interviewed Tony, a 40-something guy who had been laid off from his previous position. John liked Tony immediately because Tony said all the right things. In fact, more than once during the interview, Tony looked John in the eyes and said, "My job is to make you look good." When John asked Tony a few perfunctory questions about his employment past, Tony volunteered that he had been laid off from his previous job because his ex-wife's brother had become his supervisor and it was "too uncomfortable" for everyone involved. Being divorced himself, John felt a certain kinship with Tony. So although Tony did not have experience as a manager, John was confident he had the right disposition for it.

A few months after John hired Tony, Paul asked John how things were going. He gave Paul an exhausted look before answering. "The only reason Tony's still around is because I don't have the energy to look for a replacement." Over time, John had to acknowledge that Tony just did not have the skills crucial to performing the job. Tony had a great rapport with his employees, John told me, but he could not function as a manager. The employees viewed Tony as their friend, not their boss. When Tony was asked to evaluate the performance of his 20 employees, he sent John an email that read simply, "They're all doing great work." Fine—except that John's company required detailed performance reviews of every employee. Tony also had trouble keeping up with his quarterly reports, often complaining to John that "all that paperwork is just a waste of time." John admitted that Tony had formed great relationships with his customers, but he was not fulfilling the other important requirements of the job.

The point is, in the long run, this type of mistake will cost John and his company time and money, both of which he will have to spend either to retrain Tony or to recruit, hire, and train a new employee.

To sum up, two of the most common mistakes managers make when hiring new employees are:

- Asking questions about nonmeasurable qualities
- Relying on instinct when hiring

As you've seen in the examples so far, these mistakes are costly. To prevent these common problems, you need to approach interviewing differently. In the next section you will find a process that will enable you to evaluate potential employees based on the *Core Tasks* of the position.

A DIFFERENT WAY TO INTERVIEW

There are four types of information you need to gather in an interview, and each category of questions allows you to gain insight into whether or not the candidate would be successful in the given position. Here are the question categories:

1. Credentials
2. Experience
3. Opinion
4. Behavior-Based

1. Credentials

Credentials questions target the education of potential employees; they reveal degrees, licenses, and certifications they hold.

Sample Credentials Questions

- "What level of education have you completed?"
- "What type of degree do you have?"
- "What was your GPA?"
- "Do you have any special certifications?"
- "Would you be willing to take a math/reading/computer literacy test?"
- "Have you taken any courses in computers/management/finance?"

2. Experience

Experience questions address the types of positions and range of responsibilities potential employees have held in the past.

Sample Experience Questions

- "What were your responsibilities at your previous position?"
- "How many years have you been selling software (or teaching kindergarten, etc.)?"
- "How many people do you manage in your current position?"
- "What types of accounts have you dealt with in the last three years?"
- "What are the sizes of the budgets you have managed?"
- "How many accounts do you usually handle at a given time?"

3. Opinion

Opinion questions get to the heart of the beliefs and personality of potential employees. These questions will help you determine whether an individual will be a good fit in your company's culture.

Sample Opinion Questions

- "What would you say is your greatest strength?"
- "What do you think is your major weakness?"
- "What do you like most about your job?"
- "Where do you want to be three years from now?"
- "What would you do if . . . (describe a situation that would require quick thinking)?"

Up to this point, you have probably been thinking that these are the types of questions you would normally ask. And you are right—these are the kinds of questions most interviewers ask. It's true they can give you insight into a potential employee's background and personality, but they do not really address the core competencies needed for any position. In order to determine whether or not a candidate possesses the ability to succeed at your company, you need to add a fourth category of questions to your interview repertoire.

4. Behavior-Based

Behavior-Based questions focus on the core competencies a job candidate needs to be successful in the job you need to fill. They are different from the first three categories in that they target past behaviors by asking specific questions about results, accomplishments, and outcomes. One of the outstanding benefits of Behavior-Based Questions is that they give potential employees a valuable opportunity to give you examples of their accomplishments in detail. The more specifics potential employees provide you, the better your chances of accurately evaluating whether they have the skills needed for the job.

Another perk of Behavior-Based Questions is that they can isolate the difference between aptitude and effort. For instance, Paul knows a woman who trained for years to run in the Olympics. She ate all the right foods, hired a trainer, and went to the track every day. However, she never made it to the Olympics because though she had the desire she did not have the innate talent to be a top-tier runner. This woman put forth tremendous amounts of effort, but she just did not have the aptitude to achieve her chosen goal.

This happens in business all the time. A salesman might be an extremely hard worker but might not have the personal qualities it takes to keep clients happy. If you asked him in an interview about how much effort he put forth, you would get a very positive impression of him. If, then, you asked him how much new business he closed in the past year and how he did it, you would get a very different impression.

Behavior-Based Questions reveal a greater depth of information because they ask specifics about how an individual has dealt with adversity, achievement, and other incidents in the past. As Dr. Phil McGraw has said many times on his television show and in his books, "The biggest predictor of future performance is past behavior."

Behavior-Based Questions should be crafted to deal with the Core Tasks of the position. They are not hard to create, but they take some practice because of the careful way you will need to present them. The process for using Behavior-Based Questions can be remembered with the acronym SPAR,* which stands for *situation, problem, action,* and *result.*

> **Situation:** Give an example of a Core Task of the job—"Think of a time when you were talking with a customer."
>
> **Problem:** Present a challenge or barrier to overcome in relation to the Core Task—"You had to tell the customer no."
>
> **Action:** Ask about the steps taken to rectify the problem—"What did you do in that instance?"
>
> **Result:** Learn the outcome of the problem—"Was the customer satisfied with your help?"

This type of question allows you to delve into potential employees' past actions—to see how they handled adversity, what steps they took to fix the problem, and how the overall situation was resolved. From their answers, you can determine whether or not they have the skills you have deemed necessary for the Core Task at hand.

Let's look at more examples of Behavior-Based Questions for a variety of jobs. The SPAR scenario goes like this:

> **S:** "Think of a time when you lost a sales opportunity."
>
> **P:** "Why did the customer decide not to buy?"
>
> **A:** "How did you respond to this situation?"
>
> **R:** "What was the ultimate result? What do you think you could have done differently?"

More SPAR-style interview scenarios:

- "Describe for me a situation in which you became displeased with one of your employees. What did you do to rectify the situation? How was the situation resolved?"

---

* The SPAR technique has been adapted from the commonly used STAR technique.

- "Can you think of a time when you helped someone on your team to complete a project? What part of the task did you do? How was the project received?"

- "Tell me about a situation where you didn't have enough time to complete a project. How did it happen that you ran out of time? What did you do to try and complete the project on time? How did the project turn out?"

- "Can you give me an example of a time when you saw something that needed to be changed at one of your previous jobs? Did you tell anyone about this? Was this change ever put into place? What was the result?"

Helpful Hints for Using Behavior-Based Questions

Listen for the Answer. This is one of the more difficult aspects of working with Behavior-Based Questions because it requires you to sit back and wait for job candidates to answer. Behavior-Based Questions often take interviewees by surprise, and many stumble or stare off into space while thinking of their answers. Most interviewers make the mistake of not waiting long enough for an answer, because they are uncomfortable with long silences. No matter how uncomfortable the silence, though, you must wait for the potential employee to answer. Let the person know he or she can have as much time as needed, then sit back and *listen!*

Focus on Actions. When interviewees are asked Behavior-Based Questions, they often try to sidestep the question by saying things like:

- "If that were to happen . . ."
- "In those situations, I usually . . ."
- "Most of the time I would . . ."
- "I think I might . . ."

These are typical responses, but you are not looking for what someone "might" do; you are trying to find out what they *did* do. If this happens to you—and invariably it will—you must refocus the potential employee on actions rather than speculations. Just like waiting for an answer, trying to get someone to refocus his or her answer is difficult. You might feel as if you are interrogating potential employees by pushing them to clarify. To avoid that, ask these questions as follow-ups to the Behavior-Based Questions:

- "Give me an example of when this happened . . ."
- "Can you think of a specific instance when something like this happened to you?"
- "What has been your experience when that has happened?"
- "Think of a time when you encountered this type of problem."
- "What have you done in situations like those you describe?"

At other times, potential employees will answer a Behavior-Based Question with a specific response, but they will not provide enough information for you to fully understand their actions. In these cases, you can use other types of follow-up questions to get better details. Here are some examples:

- "What was the cause of this problem?"
- "What was your role in this project?"
- "Why did you take those actions?"
- "What were the steps you took to resolve this problem?"
- "How did you tackle the problem?"
- "What was the situation's ultimate outcome?"
- "Was the client satisfied with the project?"
- "What do you think you could have done differently?"
- "How would you rate your response to this situation?"
- "If you could go back and change something, what would it be?"
- "How did your experience with this problem affect the way you dealt with future problems of the same type?"

If you ask potential employees several follow-up questions and they still do not give you the information you need, it's possible that they're holding back details. Then you must ask *yourself* some questions, to try and determine why they seem to be responding less than truthfully to you.

Next, you will read the transcripts from two sessions in which the interviewer used Behavior-Based Questions during interviews with candidates who were vying for the position of staff reporter on a metropolitan newspaper. Following each session, we'll give you our evaluations of the interviewee's responses.

Session 1: Amy

Interviewer: Amy, I am so glad you were able to meet with me today. I'm really excited to ask you some questions about your past experiences in order to better understand your skills and abilities. One of the Core Tasks of a staff reporter is to ask people uncomfortable questions. Does that make sense to you?

Amy: Of course. After all, you have to ask crime victims questions about their assaults, and you ask politicians questions about corruption. It makes perfect sense to me that an important part of a reporter's job would be to ask people uncomfortable questions.

Interviewer: Amy, I'm glad to hear you say that. Okay, tell me about a time when you had an important story to cover and you had to ask someone an uncomfortable question that he or she didn't want to answer. What did you do in that situation, and what was the outcome?

Amy: Well, let's see. That's a tough question in itself! I'll have to think about it.

Interviewer: Go ahead, take your time. I know it's a complicated question. Just think about it for a minute or two.

Amy: Hmm, well . . . Let's see. I can remember this one instance when I had to interview a woman whose husband had been killed by an armed robber during a bank holdup. She was really devastated, poor thing. She was crying, and extremely distraught. I felt uncomfortable, but I plowed through it.

Interviewer: What happened, exactly?

Amy: I was at her house doing the interview, and all of her relatives were around. In fact, the house was full of people, and here I was trying to do an interview. So, I asked her a few questions about how she met her husband. She gave me some information, but then she started crying uncontrollably and left the room.

Interviewer: That must have been really tough for you. What did you do next?

Amy: I waited a few minutes for her to come back. Then I just apologized to her family and left the house.

Interviewer: Well, how did your article turn out in the end?

Amy: It still turned out really well. I got a lot of information from the police reports to supplement the information I got from the widow.

Interviewer: Now that you can look back on it, is there anything you wish you had done differently?

Amy: No, not really.

After a few more questions, the interviewer decided to end the interview.

Interviewer: Well Amy, thanks so much for your time; it was wonderful to meet you.

Our Evaluation: The interviewer should listen not only to what Amy said but to what she did *not* say, as well. She did not say that she was determined to get the information, and she did not say that she went back the next day to ask the widow further questions. Instead, she admitted to leaving after the widow began crying, and to using the police reports rather than investigating another angle for the story. Thus, because the interviewer was looking for an investigative reporter, we conclude that Amy was not a good fit for the job. She was too easily discouraged to do the type of work needed for this position.

Session 2: Deanna

Interviewer: Deanna, I'm so glad you were able to meet with me today to interview for the staff reporter position. I'm really excited to ask you some questions about your past experiences, in order to better understand your skills and abilities. One of the Core Tasks of a staff reporter is to ask people uncomfortable questions. Does that make sense to you?

Deanna: Sure, asking people tough questions is part of the job. If you don't ask tough questions, you'll never be a good reporter.

Interviewer: That sounds good, Deanna. My question has to do with your past experiences. Can you give me an example of a time when you had to ask someone an uncomfortable question that he or she didn't want to answer? What did you do in that situation, and what was the result?

Deanna: Well, let me think for a minute. I ask people questions every day, but a lot of times they *want* to talk to me.

Interviewer: Just take as long as you need.

Deanna: Last year, there was a case in which a man was arrested for selling drugs. One of his customers died because the drug was laced with something deadly. I decided I wanted to interview the drug dealer's mother; she'd been living in a house her son had paid for in cash, and she drove around town in a brand-new car. I called her to set up the interview, and she said she'd be happy to talk with me. When I got to her house, however, she told me she'd changed her mind. I convinced her to let me come in for just a minute. Once I was inside, I decided I wasn't leaving until I got that interview. First I complimented her on her house. I noticed the built-in bookshelves she had in her living room, and I asked her if she had put them in herself. She started telling me about the books she collected and the imported figurines she had displayed throughout her home. As she became more comfortable with me, I started to introduce the topic of her son. I mentioned how difficult it must be for a mother to see her son pursue illegal activities. I asked her what type of child he had been and what activities he had liked when he was little. She told me how he loved to draw when he was younger, but that he had gotten in with some other kids who were troubled. Then she just opened up to me. She explained that he had disappeared for a while when he was in his twenties. When he came back, she thought he'd changed. He had a job and offered to pay her mortgage. She had been able to quit her job and take care of her sick mother. By the time she figured out what he was up to, selling illegal drugs, it was too late. Finally, I asked her about her son's customer who had overdosed. At that point, she broke down. She told me she felt terribly guilty, that she had just that morning called a real estate agent about selling the house and leaving town. She said that she knew what her son had done was wrong, and that she had wanted to call the mother of the boy who died, but her son's lawyer had told her not to do it.

Interviewer: How did the story turn out?

Deanna: I turned it into a series of articles, which were really well received. More importantly, though, I learned that being genuinely interested in people helps me interview them more effectively.

Interviewer: Deanna, thanks so much for sharing that story with me. I'd like to ask you a few more questions, if that would be okay.

Our Evaluation: Obviously, Deanna was someone who had at least two of the skills needed to be a great reporter: She was willing to pursue people who did not want to answer her questions, and she found a way to get them to talk without being confrontational or pushy. Deanna had learned a technique that enabled her to be successful as an interviewer. The interviewer would still have to evaluate whether or not Deanna had the other skills needed to be the new staff reporter, but she certainly would be one of the top candidates.

This type of interviewing takes time, but it pays huge dividends in the long run, as it helps you weed out potential employees who would be unmotivated or difficult to manage in the future. This also prevents you from making a mistake like the one at the beginning of the chapter when a company lost money by hiring someone who could not or would not succeed. This type of interviewing may not come naturally at first, but after practice you will see that your interviews are more focused and much more effective. As a result, your company will be populated by motivated, skilled and hard-working employees.

For more information on topics discussed in this chapter, visit our website at: www.questionsthatgetresults.com/hiring.

CHAPTER 7

Questions That Uncover Goals

How can you inspire your employees if you have not yet identified your own professional and personal goals? If you can do that first, you will be better able to help your employees achieve their own goals, while making sure theirs align with yours. This alignment is crucial, because without it, you and your employees might be working at cross-purposes.

When Paul started out in the sales industry, he got a job working for a manager we will call Larry. At the time, Paul was insecure about his sales skills and wanted someone who could mentor him and offer advice when he needed it. Little did Paul realize, Larry's goal was to retire in three years. He focused all his time and energy on this goal. When Paul asked him for advice on how to approach potential clients, he shrugged. "You know, Paul, I really don't know. I was hoping you'd have some answers." At that moment, Paul knew he had to look for another job, because one of his goals at the time was to find a mentor, to learn from someone with experience in the industry. Mentally, Larry had already left the working world behind; now his attention was centered on his impending retirement, in a nice house adjacent to a golf course. Much as Paul liked Larry, their conflicting goals made it impossible for them to work together.

Before going any further, let us discuss the definition of a goal. You might think it is silly to even try to define what a goal is, and that is okay. We used to think we knew how to define the term until we spoke to motivational coach Michael Wickett. Mike told us that only 2 percent of the population has goals. With that, a debate ensued.

We told Mike, "When we ask salespeople at our seminars, 'Who here has goals?,' they all raise their hands."

He shook his head. "No, guys, they don't have goals. They have *dreams.*"

That puzzled us. "What's the difference?"

"Dreams are in your head. Goals are written down," Mike explained. "In order for something to be a goal, you need to write it down."

We soon realized Mike was right. Many people have dreams about how they want their lives to unfold, but few people take the time to sit down and form detailed plans to make their dreams a reality. Think about it this way: How many people do you know who would like to be in better physical shape? The older we get, the more we think about getting healthier, and for many of us, losing weight is a giant step in that direction. Now consider how many people have actually made losing weight one of their life goals. Sure, plenty of us *want* to lose weight, but how many of us really put that dream into action in the form of a solid goal, with specific steps for reaching it?

HOW TO TURN YOUR DREAM INTO A GOAL

There are four "musts" for turning your dream into a goal:

1. *A goal must be written down.* The process of writing down your goals forces you to turn your vague desires into concrete objectives.

2. *A goal must be specific.* By ensuring that your goals are specific, you can focus your energy and thus maximize how you spend

your time. Rather than saying, "I want to make my life better," set specific goals such as, "I want to own a home," or "I want to be happily married."

3. *A goal must be measurable.* If your goals are not measurable, you will not know whether or not you have reached them. An example of a measurable goal might be, "I want to lose 15 pounds," or "I want to sell $2 million worth of products."

4. *A goal must have a time frame.* You have to define your goals in terms of time; otherwise, you might put them off indefinitely. The time frame for one of your goals could be anywhere from 1 week to 20 years, or more. The important thing is to have a deadline—and stick to it!

Here are some examples of personal and professional goals that meet all four of these requirements:

- "My goal is to lose 15 pounds in the next six months."
- "I have a goal to make $2 million in the next fiscal year through sales of my new product."
- "My goal is to own a three-bedroom vacation home at the beach two years from today."
- "I have a goal to open up 15 new franchise locations of my business in the next five years."

Now that you know the difference between goals and dreams, the next step is to do a personal inventory. What are your goals? You want to have a clear direction of where you want yourself, and those you manage, to go. This will help maximize your efforts and determine what you need from your employees. The following questions will help you with that process.

Questions to Help You Delineate Your Goals

- "What's my vision of the future?"
- "Where do I picture myself three years from today?"

- "How do I want others to perceive me in the future—my boss, my peers, my family?"
- "What has to happen in the next two years for me to be happy with my progress?"
- "What visual image do I have for my team? What visual image do I have for my company?"
- "How do I want to be perceived by my customers? My employees?"
- "How would my boss describe me in one sentence?"
- "What are they (employees, customers, boss, peers) saying about me now? What would I like them to say three years from now?"
- "Which mountain do I want to climb?"
- "What's my definition of success?"
- "What benchmarks do I need to meet in order to feel successful?"

Take some time to think about your own goals, then follow the aforementioned guidelines and write down some of your personal and professional goals. As we said at the beginning of the chapter, once you know what you want, you will be better prepared to help your employees figure out what they want.

As managers, many of us assume that our employees already have goals they are working toward in their careers and personal lives. We take for granted that the people working for us have identified clear short-term and long-term objectives, and that each day they are working to further those objectives. If we opened our eyes a little wider, however, we would notice that certain employees seem to be more driven and focused than others. To see these differences more clearly, it helps to think of our employees as occupying a three-tier system.

- On the bottom tier are those employees with whom we spend much of our time. They need constant guidance, discipline, and supervision. Often, our bottom-tier employees do not really have the qualifications or experience they need for their jobs.

- On the top tier are our best performers, those employees who achieve above and beyond our expectations. Top-tier employees get all the glory in our business because they excel consistently, even in tough situations.

- On the middle tier are the employees who do what they are asked to do, but that's about it. It's the employees on this tier that we'll spend much of our time discussing in this chapter. Ordinarily, these employees do not get a lot of face time with their managers. They generally don't "rock the boat" and so are not seen as problem workers. They come in on time and they get their work done. They may not necessarily take on leadership roles, and they do not always go out of their way to bring the company business. Often, they have the potential to do much more, but for one reason or another choose not to do so.

As managers, it is in our best interest to push middle-tier employees to stretch their limits and create goals for themselves. Unfortunately, many managers fail to do this because of the time involved in turning an average employee into a superstar. This is a mistake, for if we can encourage an employee to climb from the middle tier to the top tier, it will result in company growth, raise morale, and improve the performance of other employees who spot the potential for advancement.

UNDERSTANDING EMPLOYEES ON THE MIDDLE TIER

Here is an example of what *usually* happens with middle-tier employees: Nancy has been a salesperson for four years, and in her performance reviews, she's invariably described as "loyal, dependable, and hard-working." She's firmly entrenched on the middle tier of salespeople, and she does not seem to mind. Her manager, Sue, is about to conduct Nancy's annual review. Sue knows Nancy is smart and capable of doing much better, but she doesn't want to push the issue because she doesn't want to risk offending Nancy and, thus, increasing the chances she might quit. As her manager, Sue has enough on her plate dealing with salespeople who *need* to be replaced because of their repeated failure to reach their quotas. Nancy, in contrast, has always been able to hit her targets, but she's just not all that interested in expanding her customer base or motivating her existing customers to buy more.

On the day of Nancy's review, Sue spends her morning putting out fires started by one of her salespeople who did not follow through on an order. Now, as she looks over Nancy's file, she resigns herself to the fact that Nancy is a middle-of-the-road employee. Still, during their meeting, she asks Nancy if there is anything she can do to help her, to which Nancy replies that things are going well. But when Sue asks about raising Nancy's quota for the next quarter, Nancy balks. She tells Sue that in this market there's no way she can meet an increase in her quota. Furthermore, she tells Sue that she has family commitments that prevent her from working overtime. At this point, Sue tries to give Nancy a pep talk, taking care to highlight Nancy's potential, but by the end of the meeting, it's clear that Nancy intends to continue in her role as a middle-tier employee.

As managers, most of us can see ourselves in Sue's situation. We know there's untapped potential in many of our employees; we just do not know how to tap into it. This is where the importance of asking the right questions comes into play. In this story, Sue tried to discuss Nancy's mediocre performance with her, but she failed to ask the right questions. This often happens when employees give us excuses as to why they cannot do better. Nancy talked about tough market forces, as well as her commitment to her family. These are both legitimate issues, and so we, as managers, tend to accept them at face value. Yet, keep in mind that top-tier employees produce in the face of these same issues. They have families, too; and they're affected by the economy. What can we do to help our middle-tier employees reach for the top level? In order to spur them to greatness, we need to uncover their goals, or help them create goals if they do not already have them.

The first action to take is to guide employees through a goal-setting process. Give them the following assignment a week before their performance review and instruct them to have it ready when you two meet.

Assignment: First, think about your future and what you really want to accomplish in your life. Then, for each of the following eight areas, write out your immediate and long-term goals. Make sure that each of these goals is measurable, specific, and has a time frame. Once you've written out your goals, number the areas in order of importance, with 1 being most important and 8 being least important. During your performance review next week, we'll discuss these goals. Here are the eight goal categories:

1. Career
2. Family
3. Finance
4. Health
5. Personal growth
6. Recreation
7. Social/community
8. Spiritual

A word of caution: I realize that asking your employees about their spiritual, family, health, and even recreational goals may be controversial. Some of them will not want to share these areas of their lives with you, and that is perfectly acceptable. These topics can be very sensitive for people, for a variety of reasons, and many managers are uncomfortable talking about such personal issues. Certainly employees have the right to keep their personal lives private from their bosses. As a manager, however, you need to be ready and willing to discuss these topics if an employee is willing to do so.

For many of our employees, their families and/or their spiritual practices make up a large part of their lives. If you do not give them the opportunity to discuss these important subjects with you, you risk that they might feel isolated or misunderstood. Best-selling authors like Dale Carnegie, Norman Vincent Peale, Steven Covey, and Tony Robbins all urge their readers to address spiritual goals along with financial, career, and family goals.

You can put your employees at ease during this discussion by telling them this before they make out their list: "Nothing you say in this meeting will be held against you. If you list your career as one of your less important goals, that is okay. I simply want to get information from you that will help us, together, set professional goals for you, goals that align with those of our company and mine as a manager."

Many people believe a person's goals need to balance; we do not. Let's face it, at different stages of your life, different areas will require more of your attention. For example, when you have young children, there is no question that you will need to direct more of your time and energy on your family goals. As your children grow up and leave home, you can then transfer some of that energy into your career goals. Or if you have a sick family member, you might have to take time away from work to focus entirely on your family. On the other hand, if you are up for a promotion, or if you are starting your own business, you might inform your family that you will be virtually unavailable for a certain period of time—pointing out that the results will end up benefitting all of you. And, if you get sick, of course you'll need to make your health your number-one priority.

What emerges from this goal exercise should be a ranking of your employee's priorities. Another word of warning here: Be prepared to hear statements you might not want to hear. An employee might tell you that his family and health are his top two priorities, and that his career is currently last on his list. Nevertheless, he still can have career goals that you can help him meet. (He has to continue working, after all, to pay bills and/or keep his family afloat.)

After your employees have completed the assignment, it is time for you to ask them some questions. As a manager, you will naturally want to pay close attention to each employee's career and finance goals, but it's crucial not to neglect the other areas! Here are some sample questions to ask:

- "Which area did you rank as number one? Why is that area so important to you?"
- "What are your long-term career goals?"

- "What are your immediate career goals?"
- "When you think about your long-term financial goals, do they seem to be in synch with your career goals?"
- "Do any of your goals conflict with one another?"
- "What do you see as some of the barriers to your goals?"
- "Describe for me the effort it will take to achieve these goals. How does that compare with what you are currently doing?"
- "In what ways are you currently on track to achieve all your goals?"
- "Do you currently have all the resources you need to meet your career goals?"
- "What must happen at this time for you to be able to move forward to reach your financial goals?"
- "What's your action plan for your career goals? How do you hope to accomplish the goals you've set for yourself?" (Don't expect an immediate answer to this question. Your employees will need time to think about their plan and write it out. Instruct them to include the following in their action plan:
  - The ultimate goal of the plan
  - The resources they will need to complete the plan, and the process by which the plan will be carried out

Once your employees have written out their plan, your next step is to ask how they plan to implement it.

Inevitably, once your employees have written their action plans they will expect some assistance or additional resources from you, the team, or the company. Be prepared to work with them and do as much as you can to help them succeed.

Below is another exercise you can instruct your employees to complete to help them delineate their goals. This one is especially beneficial for those employees who seem to be wandering aimlessly at work.

Assignment: Imagine it's five years in the future, and you're wildly successful. All the things you hoped for in your career have come true. Write a letter of appreciation to each of the people who helped you make your dreams come true. Make sure to thank *all* of the individuals who contributed to your success, and give examples of the assistance they provided you, whether it was a grand gesture or a small act of kindness.

Once your employees have completed the letter of appreciation, ask them three questions:

1. "Who did you thank in your appreciation letter?"
2. "What help did each of those people give you?"
3. "What were you able to achieve as a result of their help?"

This exercise helps your employees understand on a deeper level what they want in the future; at the same time, it allows you to determine what type of assistance and resources they will need to achieve those goals.

Patrick and his wife first came across this type of goal-setting exercise many years ago when their kids were very little and he was deeply involved in building his career. Patrick was working four nights a week, in addition to five days a week. His wife stayed home with their two children. Patrick called home one Friday night and told his wife he once again would not be able to make it home that night before the kids went to bed. His wife became furious.

"Honey, wait a minute," Patrick said gently. "We wrote out our goals, and we agreed that this was important for me, remember? I need to have this project succeed in order to get a promotion; and in the long run, that'll help you and the kids, too, not just me."

She apologized. "You're right, Patrick. I admit I'm disappointed, and upset, that you won't be home tonight, but I know this is a sacrifice we both have to make."

The next morning—Saturday—Patrick desperately wanted to sleep late. He was exhausted from the previous week. His wife came in at 8:00 AM and woke him up. Patrick grumbled that he was tired. Now it was her turn to remind him of their mutual goals.

"Now, wait a minute, honey," she said. "We agreed long ago that Saturdays are supposed to be family days. When we set our goals, we promised not to let work interfere with spending one day a week together, as a family." Patrick knew she was right, and so he got up to go spend the day with his family. Sure, he was tired, but he did not regret it, and they ended up having a great day together. Because Patrick and his wife had set these goals in advance, it was easier for them to work together and not be pulled apart.

This is the power of goals, they can help eliminate conflict and encourage short term sacrifice for long term gain. Once you and your employees recognize each other's goals and the steps needed to achieve them, you can work towards meeting those goals together.

CHAPTER 8

Questions That Manage Across

$\mathbf{A}$s managers, we get used to telling people what to do, how to do it, and when to do it. We give instructions to the employees we manage and, for the most part, those employees do what we ask of them. Difficulties can arise, however, when we have to work with people who do not report directly to us, and we have to depend on their assistance to get our jobs or projects done. Whether they are employees who work in a different department or other managers in our company, what happens when we need something to be done, and the person on the other end does not want to do it? Or, he or she agrees to do it but then fails to follow through? Or, the person does it on his or her timeline, which does not mesh with ours?

In many companies, this problem arises more often than we would like to imagine. Departments may have developed adversarial relationships over time or have conflicting priorities and goals. Sometimes the issue is limited resources and not enough staff available to complete projects. Or, there might be a lack of guidance from the directors and, therefore, departments have too much autonomy and no clear guidelines on how to work together. Even at the top, vice presidents or senior managers may refuse to help one another, and as a result, resources get wasted, productivity drops, and customers suffer because their needs are not being met adequately by the company.

As a manager, what can you do when someone at your own company is making your job more difficult? In our many years of leadership training, we have noticed that most people in such a situation choose one of the following options:

- Complain to their boss.
- Try to nudge the employee gently into helping.
- Confront the employee, even if it escalates to a shouting match.
- Try to work around the employee who is erecting the obstacle.
- Suffer through without saying a word.
- Give up on projects and opportunities that involve that employee.

Unfortunately, most of these options are not successful. Quite the opposite, in fact; often, they lead to more conflict and hardening of battle lines.

Instead of plowing these predictable paths, you can choose to do something different. You can find a way to rectify the situation so that your life and job will be easier; equally important, you will be able to demonstrate how vital you are to the company. In this book, we call this strategy *managing across,* to reflect the fact that you are transferring those skills you use as a manager (such as motivation, negotiation, and organizational management) to forge a new relationship with one of your fellow managers or an employee in another department.

In this chapter, we present you with two examples of situations when you can use this managing-across technique. In the first example, you will learn how to rectify a one-time problem that arises between your department and another department in your company. The second example will illustrate how to solve an ongoing issue between two departments in a way that addresses the underlying causes of the problem and ultimately changes the circumstance for the better. Throughout both examples, we will provide you with the questions you will need to ask in order to determine the best course of action to take when you have to manage across situations.

MANAGING ACROSS: A ONE-TIME PROBLEM

Mark and Rich work for the same multinational scale company. Mark has been with the company for 34 years and currently holds the position of regional service manager. He oversees 40 service technicians who provide routine maintenance and troubleshooting services to companies throughout the northeastern United States. Rich has been with the company for three years and works as a salesman in the same region as Mark.

In September, Mark takes a call from a longtime customer who tells him that his 30-year-old truck scale (which Mark installed) finally needs to be replaced. Mark has a long-established relationship with this customer and knows the customer trusts him. The customer asks Mark what he needs to do, and Mark tells him the exact specifications for the new scale. He then instructs the customer to call Rich to order the new scale, explaining that his company does not allow him to process sales transactions.

The new scale will cost the customer approximately $75,000 and earn Rich a commission of $1,500. Mark will not get a commission off this sale, but he will earn a bonus of $150 from the new service contract the customer will sign upon delivery of the new scale. To Mark, it seems as though he has handed this sale to Rich on a silver platter; in his mind, Rich did not have to lift a finger to make a $1,500 commission.

On the day of the delivery of the new truck scale, both Mark and Rich are present at the customer's site. Once the scale is installed, the customer looks to Mark and asks, "Where is the new printer?" (Truck scales provide a printout of the weight of each truck they weigh.) Mark looks to Rich, who says, "The customer didn't order a printer."

Here's the problem: Usually, printers are ordered along with any new truck scale, but this customer did not specifically ask for one, and Rich failed to suggest one while the transaction was being made. Mark sees this as Rich's mistake; specifically, that a salesperson working for the company for any length of time should be familiar with the scales and know that truck scales require printers. A new printer usually retails for $500, but the customer contends he has already paid enough money for the scale, moreover, he just wants the scale up and running—now!

At this point, Mark and Rich excuse themselves from the customer. Immediately, Mark asks Rich, "Why didn't you put the printer on the purchase order with the new scale?" Rich replies, "The customer never asked for a printer, so I didn't order one. Now we're going to have to get another purchase order and ask him to cut us a check for $500 so we can get this printer." Mark is taken aback. He cannot believe Rich wants to charge this longtime customer an additional $500 for the printer. He tells Rich, "This was your mistake. You never even mentioned the printer, so he assumed he was going to get one with the scale. Your job as a salesperson is to make sure you have covered all your bases before you finalize any transaction. And you didn't do that. The money for the new printer should come out of your commission." Rich balks at that suggestion and walks away, leaving Mark to deal with the customer.

Mark goes back inside to find the customer is furious. He tells Mark, "I just spent $75,000 for a truck scale that is worthless unless I have a printer." Mark wants to agree with the customer, but he stops himself. Instead, he says, "Give me 24 hours to work this out for you." The customer agrees, reluctantly, and Mark heads back to his office.

How can Mark resolve this situation? He cannot order Rich to give the customer a printer—Rich does not work for him. Mark does not want to make an enemy out of Rich, but he does not want to anger a longtime customer, either. To make the best of this bad situation, Mark should use the managing-across technique of questioning to uncover Rich's motivations and, ultimately, make a deal that will work for both of them.

Here is the way managing across this situation might play out:

Mark: Rich, I really need to talk to you about this printer situation.

Rich: That guy is not getting a $500 printer for free.

At this point in the conversation, the two men could easily become confrontational. Mark could blame Rich for not doing his job, and Rich could counter that it is easy for Mark to say he should give up his commission, since Mark is salaried and Rich is not. Instead, Mark chooses to ask questions and get to the root of the problem.

Mark: I understand you are frustrated. *How do you think we should handle this?*

Rich: I think he needs to cut us a check for $500 and then we'll order him a new printer.

Mark: He seemed pretty adamant that he wasn't going to give us $500 for the printer. Understandably, he is upset that he has a $75,000 truck scale just sitting there doing nothing. He is a businessman who is trying to run his business. *What do you think is fair?*

Rich: Hey, whoever said life was fair? My commissions are getting smaller every year, and this economy is not helping. My boss is breathing down my neck every quarter to meet my quota, and he would just ream me out if he thought I made a mistake with this sale.

Mark: Rich, I understand. I feel the same pressure you do. *What can I do to make this easier?*

Rich: Maybe you can talk to the customer; he trusts you.

Mark: Okay, I can talk to him. But I need to be able to offer him something. He is pretty ticked off right now. I don't think we can expect him to pay full price for the printer at this point. *What can we do to make everyone happy?*

Rich: Well, the wholesale price of the printer is only $250. I guess we could let him have it for that price. That way the company does not lose any money. Of course, I'll have to explain to my boss why I'm essentially giving a printer away.

Mark: Maybe you can tell your boss that you discounted the printer because the guy went with the top-of-the-line scale. *Would you be happy with that arrangement?*

Rich: I guess I could live with that. Will you talk to the customer?

Mark: I will. I'll apologize for the misunderstanding and tell him that we'll give him the printer for half price, and that we'll ship it to him overnight. I'll make sure that one of my guys is there to install it first thing in the morning. He is a reasonable guy, and I am sure he will be fine once the printer is there and the scale is up and running.

Unquestionably, throughout this conversation, Mark took the high road. He did not get drawn into a disagreement with Rich, and he did not make demands. Instead, he asked Rich a series of questions that helped him to find out where Rich was coming from and what he was willing to do to resolve the problem. In this way, Mark was able to broker a compromise, enabling everyone to walk away feeling like they had been heard.

It is important to point out that each party in this scenario had to give a little. Rich had to sell the customer a printer at cost; Mark had to soothe Rich's feelings and apologize to the customer; and the customer had to pay for the printer—though he got it for 50 percent off the retail price.

Here are the steps to the managing-across technique that Mark used to solve his one-time problem with Rich:

Step 1: Ask the other person questions to find out where he or she is coming from—Mark asked Rich, "How do you think we can handle this?" When that question did not get a satisfactory response, he went further, asking Rich, "What do you think is fair?" Those questions forced Rich to explain himself and his thought process.

Other questions that could work for this step include:

- "How do you see the situation?"
- "Why do you feel so strongly about . . . ?"
- "What do you think about this issue?"

Step 2: Ask a question to align yourself with the other person, rather than against him or her—After Rich complained about his boss and the pressure of quotas, Mark had a simple way to connect with him. He asked Rich, "What can I do to make this easier?" This question disarmed Rich and allowed him to start thinking of Mark as an ally instead of an enemy.

Other options for this step would be:

- "How can I help?"
- "What do you need from me?"
- "Where can we go from here?"

Step 3: Enlist the other person in creating a plan—Mark asked Rich, "What can we do to make everyone happy?" This put the ball in Rich's court and forced him to think about a solution that would be a compromise. Mark followed up this question with another: "Would you be happy with that arrangement?" He did this to make sure that Rich felt like a partner in this plan, not an unwilling participant.

Other questions you might use for this step:

- "How can we resolve this issue?"
- "What do you see as the solution to this problem?"
- "Which way do you want to go with this?"
- "What are some other options we haven't considered?"

This step-by-step process enables you to resolve many of the controversies you will confront as a manager. Some problems between departments or managers are more entrenched, however, and require a slightly different approach.

MANAGING ACROSS: AN ONGOING PROBLEM

Our local newspaper recently ran a series of disturbing articles about backlogs in our state's DNA labs. Apparently, several violent criminals had been released from prison because DNA results had not been delivered on time to their defense attorneys and, as a result, their cases had been dismissed. As the newspaper article made clear, there was certainly enough blame to go around. To start, the judges blamed the prosecutors; apparently, there is a rule that DNA results have to be provided to the defense at least 45 days before the trial date. Prosecutors were missing these deadlines, leaving judges no choice but to dismiss the cases. In turn, the prosecutors were blaming the DNA labs for not delivering the test results to them on time. The technicians in the labs weighed in, too, claiming that they were overworked and understaffed and that the prosecutors did not give them enough prior notice to get the tests done before the trial dates. Finally, all parties mentioned in the article blamed the state for not adequately funding the labs to hire new personnel and purchase new equipment.

As we read this article, we became upset, as anyone would, but we were also curious about the working relationships between all of these departments. As we saw it, the prosecutors could certainly use the managing-across technique to coordinate with the lab technicians so that DNA results would be ready on time. Here is how that process might be accomplished:

The head prosecutor, Ann Richmond, has decided that enough is enough. She is embarrassed and angry about the series of news articles being published regarding the too-late DNA results. It's a difficult situation, for she's well aware that the state does not have the money to expand its DNA testing facilities. At the same time, she is tired of criminals going free on technicalities. Instead of blaming someone else, however, she decides to take action. She calls the manager of the state's DNA labs, James Dole, and asks him to meet her for lunch.

Ann: Well, James, that certainly was an unflattering series of articles in the newspaper.

James: Yes, it was.

Ann: I'm really frustrated with the whole situation. I realize that my prosecutors have not always done the best job of notifying your technicians about their timelines, and I apologize for that. Also, I realize you guys are swamped, and I hope the state will finally give you the extra money you need. Until that happens, though, I think it is important that we work together. *Do you think the two of us can come up with a plan to make things run more smoothly?*

James: I really hope so. I hate being made to look like the bad guy in the papers, and it makes me sick to think that there are murderers out on the streets now because of this problem.

Ann: I feel the same way you do. I think part of the problem is that my prosecutors do not understand your lab's processes. *Can you explain to me how things are prioritized?*

James: Well, as you said, we are severely understaffed and under-funded. We have two brand-new machines that we cannot use yet because we do not have the money to get them officially calibrated. Also, although 10 percent of our positions are vacant, we cannot hire anyone new right now because of the statewide hiring freeze. So, we work on demand—we do not start testing DNA until the prosecutor calls us to tell us a trial date has been set. This means that there is undoubtedly DNA in our labs right now that might clear some of the accused crowding our state's prisons. It also means that we can't use DNA to help catch any criminals who are still on the streets, simply because it is not being tested. Of course, as we learned last week, it also means that a guilty person can be set free because his defense attorney did not get the results of our tests in time.

Ann: I didn't realize how bad it was in your department. I had heard complaints about a lack of staff and funding, but I had no idea it was that serious. I know my prosecutors sometimes call you only a few weeks before a trial is set to start. Obviously, that is not going to fly if we need to hand the results over to the defense 45 days before the trial date. Given the fact that your department is so short-handed, I think we need to talk about a more realistic timeline. *How long does it take to process DNA?*

James: It will usually take between 5 to 10 days, depending on the amount and quality of DNA available.

Ann: Okay, so that means if it needs to be ready 45 days before the trial date, we need to give your lab close to 60 days to process DNA in order to guarantee it will be done in time. *What else do you need from us?*

James: Well, I think we need some way of knowing what priority level to assign to each case. When the prosecutors call us, they always claim that their case is the most important and needs to be "rushed." I think we need to determine some way to prioritize cases so the lab techs know which ones really need to be fast-tracked and which ones can wait.

Ann: That makes a lot of sense. What if we came up with a system that assigns priority labels to cases, such as: red = most important, yellow = moderately important, and green = least important. I could work with my prosecutors to assign the labels so that our office agrees on how they are prioritized before they are sent over to you. *Do you think we could then stipulate a number of days that each label category would typically require to be processed?*

James: I think so. We could make sure that red-level cases are completed within 6 days, yellow-level cases within 10 days, and green-level cases within 2 weeks. How does that sound?

Ann: That sounds good. Obviously, this will mean that some cases will have to take a backseat to others, but at least everyone will be aware of how cases are prioritized. So, to review, we will make sure that we give your office at least 60 days lead time before a trial starts. When we do hand over a case to one of your technicians, we will assign it a category labeled red, yellow, or green. Then your techs will make sure that the case is ready by the agreed-upon date.

James: I think that will make things run much more smoothly.

In this scenario, the issues were more complicated than in the first example. One of the lessons from this story is that, as managers, we do not have control over many of the forces that affect our jobs. In this case, the head prosecutor had no control over the budget of the DNA labs, and she could not force the state to spend more money on equipment and techs. She had to manage across by working within the limits of her position. Many managers in her place would simply have given up because they did not have control over the entire situation. What Ann did, however, was to step outside the box and empower herself to change the circumstances. This type of creative thinking would certainly get her noticed and perhaps garner a raise or a promotion.

To review, these are the managing-across steps Ann used to solve her ongoing problem with James:

Step 1: Ask for the other person's help—Ann starts the meeting by skillfully acknowledging the problem and her part in it. She also disarms James by apologizing and then sympathizing with the problems he has in his department. This makes the meeting less adversarial and, ideally, will lead to a more positive outcome. She then asks him, "Do you think the two of us can come up with a plan to make things run more smoothly?" Ann's question brings James to the table as a partner, which is critical, because without his help her problem is not going to be solved.

Other questions you could ask for this step include:

- "How can we solve this problem together?"
- "What can our departments do to work together better?"
- "What do we need to do to fix this?"

Step 2: Identify the causes of the conflict—Once Ann has enlisted James's help, she can start the process of uncovering the causes of the missed deadlines. In order to do this, she needs to understand how his department works. She asked him, "Can you explain to me how things are prioritized?" and then followed up with the question, "How long does it take to process DNA?" Ann needs this information to formulate a plan for the two departments to work together effectively.

Other question options for this step are:

- "Can you tell me more about the steps involved to process an order?"
- "How do your employees go about meeting deadlines?"
- "Where is the bottleneck in this system?"
- "Who handles those responsibilities?"

Step 3: Come up with a solution that works for both parties—Once Ann understood the lab's processes, she was better able to work with James to devise a plan that would alleviate their common problem. She made sure she got all of the necessary information by asking him, "What else do you need from us?" And after she gave him a commitment to prioritize cases, she asked for something in return, "Do you think we could then stipulate a number of days that each label category would typically require to be processed?" This sort of give-and-take ensures that each party feels like he or she is benefiting from the process.

Here are some other questions you might ask at this point:

- "What can my department or I do to ensure that the process runs more smoothly?"
- "What's an agreeable timeline for these types of projects?"
- "What's our mutual understanding about how this process will work in the future?"
- "What are some potential obstacles we need to overcome?"
- "If my department is able to do X, will your department be able to do Y?"

It may seem that this process has been oversimplified, that the problems between departments are more complicated than a few questions can solve. It is true that sometimes personal issues between managers can hinder good working relationships, and there are certainly larger organizational issues that can make it difficult for departments to work well together. However, in our experience, the way to work through these problems is by asking relevant questions. If, say, there is a personal conflict between you and another manager, the way to address it is to sit down and find out the causes of the disagreement and then determine how it can be resolved. If company issues are making things more complicated (staffing or funding conflicts, for example), you will need to coordinate with other managers on how to survive during the tough times so that your projects can still be completed on time.

It is easy to become frustrated when you believe that someone else is not doing his or her job, and is, in turn, making your job more difficult. Rather than letting that frustration fester and begin to affect your performance, it is better to implement the techniques we have presented in this chapter to help you uncover the root of the problem, along with possible solutions. Doing so not only will help you serve your customers more effectively, it will illustrate to those above and below you that you are a professional who looks for answers and solutions—that is to say, a true leader, in every sense of the word.

CHAPTER 9

Questions That Manage Upwards

We have all had those dreams where we finally get to tell our lousy bosses what we think of them. You walk right into his office and let him have it and, afterwards, walk out feeling like a million bucks. Of course, if you did that in the real world, it's more likely you would walk out of your boss's office unemployed. The good news is that your relationship with your boss is just that: a relationship, requiring the collaboration and input of two people. It is a relationship that can change for the better, even if it is only you who does the changing.

One of the most frequent scenarios we encounter in our training programs is the one in which people feel frustrated and hamstrung by their bosses. So many times over the years we have worked with clients who say, "If only my boss would get off my back, then I could do my job." Or, "I don't know what she wants from me—she has me going in 10 directions at once." Or, "He never gives me any feedback, so I don't know where I stand." We understand this frustration, because we too have worked for bosses who lack high-quality leadership and communication skills. We have even had bosses who are outright mean or incompetent. The purpose of this chapter, then, is to help you realize that, ultimately, you have a significant amount of power in the relationship between you and your boss.

When you hear your boss say, "I am only as good as my people," take that phrase to heart. It means that you have the ability to make your boss look great; conversely, you can also make him or her look like a fool. Even if you do not have the "world's best boss," you can still excel in your position and achieve a high level of success by optimizing your relationship with your supervisor. That is what we mean by the phrase "*managing upwards*." We will give you the tools to make the most of your relationship with your boss, to steer it in the right direction, and to garner the results you want in your career.

There are five categories into which "bad" bosses generally fall. These bosses are not necessarily bad people, however. In fact, they are often wonderful people with the best of intentions. Their management styles and skills are simply lacking in some way, and most likely, they are unaware of how they are perceived by their staff. The first step toward managing upwards is determining which of these categories best describes your boss:

Demanding: This type of boss has extremely high expectations for everyone. He or she feels that every item on the to-do list is top priority. This person also rarely compliments employees on a job well done and never thinks anyone else is working hard enough. The demanding boss works long hours and expects his or her employees to do the same.

Invisible: The invisible boss is perceived as aloof, uninterested, or too busy. As an employee, you will have a lot of independence and freedom, but you will never know whether you are doing a good job because this boss does not provide regular feedback. You cannot expect him or her to be your mentor or coach; and if you are hoping to learn on the job, you will be sadly disappointed. The invisible boss is not approachable, and if you ask for guidance on a project, you might get superficial advice or none at all.

Weathervane: The weathervane boss constantly changes directions and priorities. This kind of boss causes a lot of confusion because one week he or she tells you to focus all of your attention on discounting prices to move excess inventory, and the next week he or she is fuming because you are losing money by slashing prices. The next week, the weathervane boss insists that you focus on selling only your premium products to protect your margins, and the week after that, he or she wants you to call all your customers to maximize any possible sales. It is very hard to keep such bosses happy because you cannot predict what will be important from one day to the next. These bosses excel at brainstorming and raising a rallying cry, but they are no good at follow-through.

Overly critical: The overly critical boss is not outwardly mean, and his or her intentions may even be good. But bosses of this type have a habit of constantly correcting their employees and often come across as condescending. Employees who work under overly critical bosses rarely, if ever, receive praise. Instead, they are beaten down by criticism after criticism. You will hear this boss say, "This is what you should be doing"; or, "Here is what you're doing wrong." It is very difficult for employees of this type of boss to have a positive attitude in such a negative-feedback environment.

Micromanager: The micromanager loves doing the jobs of others and cannot relinquish control. Such bosses are very restricted as managers because they cannot delegate any responsibility, and end up taking on way too much work. Employees feel undermined and often lack confidence, because they are never allowed to complete a task. This boss may jump in to complete someone else's project, or redo it entirely after it has been submitted. The more the micromanager takes on, the less capable his or her employees feel, until the manager is forced to do everything because his or her employees have been made to feel incompetent.

You might recognize your boss in one of these five types, or maybe yours is a hybrid of two or more of these categories. Even though the personality traits that make up these types of bosses are different, the answer to how to improve your relationship with any of them is the same: *quality, two-way communication*. And the basis of this communication is asking great questions.

The natural inclination for most people is to communicate as little as possible with a bad boss. Most of us have a tendency to shy away from conflict, withdraw emotionally, and simply avoid someone who causes us grief. The problem with this approach, however, is that your boss will not change. Your situation will not improve, unless you make the first move, which is to simply open the doors of communication. Start by talking with your boss about things that are going well, or ask his or her opinion on something benign. Get him or her to open up to you on low-key topics so that when the time comes for more serious conversation, your relationship is genial instead of adversarial.

Admittedly, this first step can be difficult to take. In particular, if you work for one of the more critical-type bosses, you might be afraid to bring up any topic lest he or she start criticizing you. One of the ways to get around this is to approach your boss with good news, so that the mood of the conversation starts out positive, paving the way for the possibility of other upbeat topics to be discussed.

QUESTIONS TO ASK YOUR BOSS

Once you have opened the doors of communication, your next objective is to ask your boss the right questions so that you can determine the best way to improve your relationship. The time to do this is not when everyone is on a deadline and the stress level is high. Wait until a break in the action to make an appointment with your boss to discuss, for example, the upcoming quarter (or project, or year) over coffee. Or, you could ask your boss to lunch, to give you a chance to "pick his or her brain." Make sure to schedule the meeting far enough in advance so that you have time to prepare your questions beforehand.

When you begin your discussion, frame it in a positive way so that your boss does not get defensive or shut down emotionally. You might begin by saying something like, "I am really excited about the upcoming year. I am looking forward to working on all of the interesting projects we have planned. I wanted to ask you, which of our current projects are the most important to you?" As your boss answers, be sure to listen and watch his or her body language very closely. Is he or she energized about the new plans, or worried and stressed about possible problems? Next, it's important to ask follow-up questions, to garner more information and demonstrate how interested you are in these new plans.

This process seems simple, but many people do not realize that the projects or issues that are most important to their bosses need to become the ones that are most important to them, as well. As you will see, this does not mean you have to replace all of your own objectives with those of your boss. These questions allow you to, first, tap into your boss's main objectives and, then, once you have that information, use it to ensure that your goals for the future can also be met.

After you get your boss talking about his or her priorities, the next step is to ask more questions to help shape the role you want for yourself. For example, you might follow up the first question by asking, "You mentioned Project D as one of those that is the most important to you. I see my role in this project as A, B, and C; and here is how I think I should accomplish those tasks. Does this sound like it fits into your plan? And going forward, is there anything else about this project that I should keep in mind?" By asking these questions, you position yourself as a key player in your boss's most important project; you also clarify your boss's expectations, which will help you determine how best to meet them.

The next step is to summarize this plan of action in a written format and send it to your boss so that you both have detailed documentation of your discussion and agreement. If your boss is the type of person who often changes his or her mind, or is highly critical, you can reference this document and then ask if something has changed or if any of his or her expectations have not been met.

You should also ask your boss questions about the future. For example: "These are the objectives that I have set for my team to complete during the next three months, and these are the activities I am going to undertake to ensure that they are achieved. What do you think of this plan?" Allow your boss ample time to answer these questions, and make sure you take notes on his or her answers. If you want to earn a promotion or raise, or just want to improve your position in the company, make sure your boss knows your objectives. His or her responses to these questions will help clarify your expectations and let you know where you stand.

Next you'll find a list of three categories of questions you should ask your boss, followed by several suggestions in each category:

1. What's important to the boss:
   - "What are the critical issues we need to be working on in the immediate future? What about over the next year?"
   - "In my position, my three critical objectives are A, B, and C. Which one of these do you feel is the most important?"
   - "Which of the companywide initiatives will affect my department most in the coming months?"
   - "What are you looking to accomplish during the next quarter?"

2. Your goals/plans for the future:
   - "This is where I see myself in the next 12 months. What do I need to do to get there?"
   - "What qualities do you think I need to work on as a manager? Which benchmarks should I be looking at to let me know I am making progress?"
   - "I have some ideas on how we can increase profit in our department. May I run them by you to see if they are worth pursuing?"
   - "Right now I spend a lot of my time on paperwork, but I think my assistant manager could handle some of that responsibility. How might I delegate some of that responsibility so that I can spend more time on what you think is more important?"

- What are some of the skills I need to work on to help prepare me to advance to the next-level position?"

3. Boss's goals/measures of success:

   - "Where do you see yourself in five years?"

   - "Where do you want our department to be 12 months from now?"

   - "What can we do to make it happen and move us in that direction?"

It might seem daunting to have this type of conversation with your boss, especially if the two of you have never really sat down to talk before. Here are some points to keep in mind when you are preparing to start this type of dialogue:

1. *Do not give the impression that you do not know the major functions of your job.* When you start the conversation, state the priorities of the company or your department and then proceed from that point. We have seen too many companies where assumptions run rampant and objectives are never discussed. As a result, people work at cross-purposes, and these companies go nowhere.

2. *Do not treat these questions as a script.* Craft your own questions, using ours as a model. Make your questions open-ended, rather than "yes-or-no" type of questions. You will get much more information if you ask your boss to explain his or her answers.

3. *Discreetly hold your boss accountable.* What happens if your boss says one thing and does another? In that case, you have to reevaluate the situation. What you are really trying to get is clarity. You are aiming to understand your boss's thought process, how involved he or she is with the company, his or her level of interest in helping you achieve your goals, and whether or not he or she can give you what you want. For example, is your boss promising you a promotion that he or she does not have the power to grant? If so, it is better to know this now than to wait 10 years for a promotion that will never materialize.

4. *If you feel you cannot ask your boss these questions, figure out why.* Is it your boss, or is it that you lack self-confidence? If you never ask these questions, you will never gain any control over your career.

WHEN YOU DON'T KNOW WHAT THE BOSS WANTS

As you will see in the following example, failing to ask your boss the questions presented in the previous section can result in frustration, undue stress, and potentially the loss of your job. In the spring of 2010, we were asked to go down to Atlanta, Georgia to meet with some midlevel managers who work for a busy nonprofit hospital system. The boss, Louis, wanted us to meet with two of his managers who were having significant problems fulfilling their job requirements to his expectations. We walked into the situation not sure of what we would find, but eager to help these individuals become better managers.

First we sat down with Steve, who is in charge of Facilities Management for the hospital. His job is to make sure that hospital waste is disposed of properly, that the buildings are maintained, that each of the departments within the hospital is adequately equipped, and that these tasks are carried out in a very timely manner. Steve appeared to be deeply committed to his job. When we talked with him we learned that he has a genuine sense of purpose, and a mission for what he is doing. He works approximately 70 hours a week, and recently spent much of his vacation putting out fires at the office.

When we asked Steve what he saw as the problem, he said it was his boss. He told us that Louis thinks everything is a priority or an emergency that has to be dealt with immediately. He also said he had tried to talk with Louis, but he was unable to get through to him. Meanwhile, Steve's staff was unhappy because they were always going in several directions at once. According to Louis, however, Steve's people take advantage of him, whereas Steve contends that his employees are hard workers who are doing their best.

At first, our heads were spinning as we tried to make sense of this situation. We wondered what was really going on here. Fortunately, as we talked further with Steve, the picture began to get a little clearer. Steve's background, we learned, is in engineering, and he is a very meticulous worker. During our conversation, he told us a story about how he searched for the perfect flat-screen television to buy for his family—a process that took him three months!

Steve was promoted from within his department because he was seen as a hard worker who regularly took on more than he was asked to do. However, due to his history with the department, it was more difficult for him to project a "boss" persona, because just last year he had been one of the staff members he was now managing. Also, his tendency to take on more than his share of work made it problematic for him to delegate tasks to others. He would often be found working alongside his staff, helping them do their jobs, instead of coaching them as he should have been. Finally, his exacting nature hindered his ability to complete a "rush job," because he wanted everything to be perfect.

Steve knew that Louis was unhappy with his performance, but did not know how to rectify the situation. Steve was having a very tough time understanding how Louis wanted him to change, yet he never sat down and asked him directly. Instead, Steve continued to put in more hours, doing more of the work of others, and trying to make everything perfect.

The second manager Louis was having a problem with was Marcy, one of the hospital administrators. Prior to becoming an administrator, Marcy worked as a registered nurse. Louis had been continually disappointed with Marcy's performance. She was always quick to find reasons why things could not be done, he said, and consequently, she almost never met deadlines.

As we talked with Marcy, the origin of her problems became clearer. Although she was having a lot of trouble in her position, she was quick to defend her actions and place the blame on others. The truth, we discovered, was that Marcy was completely overwhelmed by her responsibilities, unable to delegate work to her staff, and unwilling to hold them accountable. She was also caught up in a small, departmental mind-set and could not see the big picture which Louis expected her to see.

Marcy knew that Louis was dissatisfied with her performance, and to avoid making things worse, at times she kept important information from him. For example, she told us of a recent problem that she had not shared with Louis. The hospital system provides a daycare center for its employees' children. During a routine inspection of the facility, one of Marcy's staff members found asbestos at the site. Instead of immediately notifying Louis, as she should have done, and taking action to close the daycare in order to have the asbestos removed, Marcy kept the problem to herself for weeks—to "protect" Louis, as she saw it. Unfortunately, Louis's boss found out about the discovery of the asbestos and asked Louis what was being done about it. Needless to say, Louis was completely caught off guard and embarrassed in front of his boss; he was forced to admit he did not know about the problem. By the time that Louis called us in to meet with Marcy, he was ready to fire her if she did not quickly and noticeably improve her performance.

As we thought about Steve, Marcy, and Louis, we realized that each of them saw the other as to blame for things not going smoothly. Both Steve and Marcy felt overwhelmed by their jobs and pulled in several different directions at once. Both also saw Louis, their boss, as micromanaging them and demanding too much. For his part, Louis felt that Steve and Marcy were not successfully managing their employees, and not focusing on the issues he felt were important In short, they were not meeting his expectations or deadlines. Quite possibly, Louis suspected, they were not even management material.

What we saw was a failure to communicate by all parties involved. Louis often gave out orders without seeking the input of his managers, whereas Steve and Marcy failed to get enough information from their boss to determine which projects were most important. An interesting related feature of this situation was that Louis had two other managers who reported to him, both of whom were extremely successful and happy in their positions. Louis had no complaints about these two, and they in turn rated Louis as an above-average boss. We worked out an action plan that called for Louis, Marcy, and Steve each to make changes in order to better manage themselves and their employees.

While Louis was an experienced manager who was able to get good results from other employees, his basic management style was one-size-fits-all. He tried to manage all of his employees the same way, and this tactic failed miserably when it came to Marcy and Steve. Neither of them was clear on how to make Louis happy, and he was not providing the direction they needed. We gave Louis the following prescription to improve how he managed Steve and Marcy:

1. Open regular, two-way communication with Steve and Marcy to discuss objectives, problems, and solutions.

2. Set aside time each month to coach and mentor Steve and Marcy individually to improve their respective management skills.

3. Establish clear, written priorities and expectations for Steve and Marcy, and manage them more closely than his other employees so that problems could not escalate into crises.

Next we focused on Marcy. She needed to gain much greater clarification on her boss's expectations. She wanted to do a good job, but she was too quick to pass the buck and to hide problems from Louis. In order to improve as both a manager and employee, Marcy needed to start being honest and asking for the help she so obviously needed. Here was our prescription for Marcy:

1. Set up a help network—made up of peers, subordinates, and/ or a supervisor who could help her improve her management skills—to alleviate her feeling that she was overwhelmed.

2. Ask her boss the tough, uncomfortable questions to learn what she is doing right, and wrong. Use one of her peers as a "practice buddy" with whom she could practice having those tough conversations.

3. Establish weekly communication with Louis to update him on current projects, and ask for his input with any problems. Commit to being 100 percent honest with Louis from now on.

Finally, we addressed Steve's circumstances. He was struggling because he wanted everything to be perfect, and he did not know how to prioritize Louis's demands. Steve also spent too much time doing his staff's job, instead of managing them. Here was our prescription for Steve:

1. Establish weekly communication with Louis to set goals and priorities. This communication should (1) specify which projects are most important, and (2) be written down to avoid any confusion or miscommunication.

2. Ask Louis for advice on how to better delegate departmental responsibilities. Refrain from going out in the field unless it is absolutely necessary (e.g., an employee has called out sick and there is a project that needs to be completed immediately).

3. Schedule weekly meetings with his staff to communicate with them more efficiently and effectively.

Some of these guidelines are short-term and will only be necessary until Steve and Marcy improve their managerial skills. Others, such as the weekly communications with Louis, should be ongoing, so that both Steve and Marcy are always informed about his priorities.

At times, managing your boss (e.g. managing upwards) can seem more time-consuming than managing your employees. In a way it is, because your employees are trained to listen to you, while your boss is more apt to give orders than to pursue two-way communications with subordinates. Managing upwards pays great dividends, however, when done correctly. There is nothing more powerful for your career than taking the time to ask your boss a few key questions that will make you more effective at work and steer you onto the right track.

For more information on topics discussed in this chapter, visit our website at: www.questionsthatgetresults.com/upwards.

CHAPTER 10

Questions That Develop and Sustain External Business Relationships

In the past, it was customary for companies to maintain separate sales and operations management divisions. The sales division focused on drumming up new business, prospecting, and calling on potential clients. Once a contract had been signed, it then shifted the accounts over to operations. Meanwhile, the operations division maintained these client relationships, putting out fires, assisting on technical issues, and making additions to the contract as it suited the clients' needs. As companies become more streamlined, however, they often make the decision to save money by melding the two divisions. In certain circumstances, a company will disband its sales division and turn over those responsibilities to the operations sector. The reasoning behind this move is that the operations managers already know the customers; likewise, they know the products and services the company provides, making them ideally positioned to sell to the customer in the future.

This shift may seem like a no-brainer to many executives, but it can be downright terrifying to operations managers who realize that selling is now part of their job descriptions. The last thing they want is to start sounding like a used-car salesman—"What can we do to get you in a car today?" The good news is that if you are one of these managers who suddenly has had sales added to your job description, you most likely already have a number of important skills that will help you be successful at it. When managers solicit business, they generally look for *good* business. They do not do a lot of prospecting or cold-calling; rather, they only go after business that they really want. Moreover, managers usually excel at responding to customer complaints, solving problems, and offering technical expertise. The one skill that managers may lack is the ability to shape a business relationship so that it can change and grow over time.

Just like any relationship, a business relationship takes time and effort to establish and then maintain. Salespeople frequently direct their energies to making new contacts and bringing in new clients but fail to follow through with the slower cultivation that is necessary to sustain a long-term successful business relationship. How many salespeople do you know who hand out their business cards like candy, or who send mass e-mails to prospective clients with little regard for their individual needs? Such salespeople often believe they are spending a lot of time building relationships. In reality, most of their business cards are thrown away, and many of their e-mails are deleted without being read. Unfortunately, many managers who are thrust into sales roles know only this stereotype of salespeople and therefore think they have to behave as such if they want to succeed. We are here to tell you that this is a misconception.

A good relationship, by definition, is mutual. Both parties need to put energy into the relationship if both are to benefit. If either side fails to live up to its responsibilities, the relationship will not work. Throughout this chapter, we will discuss how to establish strong business relationships and how to sustain them—even through difficult times, changes in company leadership, and conflicts between you and your clients. We will also discuss when to walk away from a potential relationship and, conversely, when to press for access to other contacts within the organization. One of our colleagues learned the second lesson the hard way last year.

Last summer, Dan did a consulting project with a major hotel organization. He and his team held a two-day workshop that focused on concepts such as prospecting to uncover new clients, asking good questions of new and existing clients, managing existing relationships, and negotiating for optimal profitability. The executives at the client's company were extremely satisfied with Dan's work and impressed with the results he and his team were able to achieve in such a short amount of time.

Following the conclusion of that successful project, the organization's president asked Dan to craft a more extensive program for implementation the following year. Dan had excellent rapport with key players in this organization and, therefore, had every reason to believe he had established a lasting relationship with this company.

What Dan did not know, unfortunately, was that soon after his first project was completed, the president of the hotel company brought a new executive onboard, a driven young man named David. Dan made the mistake of assuming that his relationship with this company was solid, so he did not make much of an effort to get to know David. He never met with David to discuss the new exec's plans for the organization, or asked how he would fit into David's vision for the future of the organization. If he had taken the time to learn more about David's involvement and his responsibilities, Dan might have discovered early just how ambitious and determined David was to make a quick and noticeable impact on the organization.

When the hotel company later requested detailed information about the second training program Dan had planned, he did not hesitate to share as much information as he had available. He divulged the goals and themes of the program, as well as an outline of the seminars. Unbeknownst to Dan, the president of the company passed on all of this information to David, who then used it to create his own internal program. As a result, when it came time to hammer out the final proposal and negotiation, Dan walked away with nothing. After all, the hotel execs figured, why would they hire Dan when they could save money by using David, a salaried employee, to organize the entire program from inside the company?

Dan's experience with this hotel organization illustrates clearly that you may think you have a great working relationship with a client, but you can never be sure—clients won't necessarily show you all their cards. This company hid crucial information from Dan and it hurt him in the end. Sadly, in business, this is an all too common occurrence. The lesson is, *never* take your existing clients for granted, and *never* assume you know all there is to know about a potential or current client.

DEVELOPING BUSINESS RELATIONSHIPS

We've all heard the real estate adage that the key to making sales is "location, location, location." Well, we are here to tell you that the key to developing lasting client relationships is "information, information, information." In a perfect world, you would win every contract for which you put in a bid. In reality, there will be many times when what you have to offer is just not a good fit for a targeted client's needs. So, before you spend significant time and resources putting together a lengthy proposal, it is your responsibility to uncover the pertinent information and study the situation—in short, do your homework.

Consider poor Dan: He lost the hotel organization's business after he had put in dozens of hours of work, hours he could have used on more beneficial ventures! When Dan calculated how much money he lost in the failed effort, he had to figure in not only the time he had spent working on *that* project, but also the time he was not able to devote to other projects—projects that might have brought in a profit.

That is why we stress the importance of gathering as much relevant information as possible prior to the actual negotiating phase. Think about it: If you are not prepared with a foundation of meaningful and accurate information, any proposal you build will be flimsy at best. Think of each piece of pertinent business information as a brick with which you are building your house (i.e., proposal). The more of this kind of strong material you have, the more solid your plan will be. You will ensure that you understand the client's specific needs and, therefore, can be fully prepared to meet those needs.

To help you address all the relevant areas of information when building a new client relationship, in the next section we provide a list of 11 categories of questions you should ask during this all-important research phase. Asking questions from each of these categories will enable you to develop a global understanding of your client and the requirements you will be expected to meet.

RESEARCHING POTENTIAL CLIENTS: QUESTIONS TO UNDERSTAND THEIR NEEDS

As a manager, you already know how to deal with customers and their problems. You may not think of yourself as a salesperson, but now you are being asked to develop customer relationships. One of the first things to remember is that you are looking for high-quality, long-term customers who will bring stability to the relationship. The questions in the 11 categories here are those you should consider asking any potential customer. They will help you not only to uncover their needs, but also to determine whether your products and services can meet those needs.

1. Questions to Understand Goals and Strategies

- "Can you tell me about the goals you want to accomplish over the next ___ months?"
- "What actions do you need to implement in order to achieve them?"
- "What is your vision of success?"
- "What hurdles do you expect to have to clear during this process?"
- "How does this project fit in with your overall company goals?"

2. Questions to Reveal Motivation

- "What do you hope to get out of this project?"
- "What are your concerns about your current situation?"

- "What is the most important aspect of this project to you?"
- "Can you walk me through why it is so important?"

3. Questions to Learn Alternatives

- "What other options are you considering?"
- "What options have you eliminated?"
- "How would you prioritize the alternatives from most attractive to least attractive?"

4. Questions to Discover Budgetary Issues

- "What are your budgetary parameters?"
- "How will money be allocated?"
- "How are budgets for this type of project determined?"
- "Can you walk me through your budget decision-making process for this type of project?"

5. Questions to Clarify the Decision-Making Process

- "Can you walk me through your decision-making process?"
- "Who, in addition to yourself, is involved in setting the criteria for this project?"

6. Questions to Determine Time Frame and Constraints

- "What is your ideal time frame for this project?"
- "What benchmarks will you set up along the way to ensure that you meet your objectives in a timely manner?"
- "In the past, what have been some of the challenges to staying on schedule?"
- "What obstacles might need to be addressed in order to move forward?"

7. Questions to Discern Consequences

- "What would be the consequences if this project did not pan out?"

- "What would be the implication to your department if you did not achieve X, Y, and Z?"
- "If your current approach does not succeed, what will be the impact on you? Your team? Your organization?"

8. Questions to Uncover Pertinent History

- "Can you describe similar projects you have worked on in the past?"
- "Of those projects, what worked? What didn't? Can you explain to me the differences between what worked and what did not?"
- "What have you learned from previous experiences in this area?"
- "Tell me what has happened in the past to plans like these?"

9. Questions to Reveal Problems

- "Can you define the problem for me? Can you give me an example?"
- "What is causing the problem?"
- "How long has it been a problem?"
- "What is the problem costing you in terms of resources, profits, overhead, customer satisfaction, delivery schedules, quality, market share, and so on?"
- "What have you done so far to address the issue?"

10. Questions to Understand Feelings and Perceptions

- "What are your feelings about this project as it gets underway?"
- "How do you think everything is progressing so far?"
- "What was your initial reaction to this idea?"
- "Do you believe this initiative can succeed?"

11. Questions to Determine Next Steps

- "What is your next step?"
- "Where do you want to go from here?"

By now you may be thinking, "These are way too many questions to ask a client who has not even committed to working with me." Don't misunderstand: You do not need to, nor should you ask *all* of these questions on your first call. Always use your common sense and adjust the type and number of questions you will ask as appropriate to the customer's level of interest and time he or she has for a conversation. Don't forget to make it personal; reveal your personality and style when you ask these questions as this will help the relationship develop over time. Remember, you are posing these questions to help establish what you hope will be a lasting relationship between you and the prospective client.

On occasion, these questions will lead to unexpected answers. You might find out that this is a dead-end client or a demanding one who will never be satisfied with any product or service you have to offer. By asking these questions, you can find out early on whether or not this is a relationship in which it will be worthwhile to invest your time, energy, and company resources. Keep in mind that the ultimate goal is to forge relationships in which you can be an advisor and a partner. The only way you do that is by asking the right questions.

HOW QUESTIONS CAN SAVE YOU TIME AND MONEY

Through our consulting work, we have encountered numerous situations in which asking the right questions has saved companies from wasting their resources on a dead-end project. We have also witnessed occasions when asking relevant, well-crafted questions resulted in increased business for our clients. Here are two of the most recent examples that show how asking questions can save money and make money.

Mitch and his team were eager to work for the Fortune 500 company that had contacted them about doing some web design projects. His team was so intent on getting their hands on the project that they neglected to inquire as to why this major corporation was ending its long-standing relationship with a well-known web design team to work instead with Mitch's little-known company. Mitch, fortunately, was not so easily distracted. Before he allowed his team to spend time developing their proposal, he insisted that they ask their contacts at this company some pointed research questions. And to ensure all the bases were covered, Mitch provided his team leader with the following list of questions to ask the potential client:

- "What is working? What is not? As to the latter, why do you think those things are not working?"
- "Tell me, what is prompting you to look at alternatives, as opposed to staying with your current situation?"
- "What is the outcome you hope to achieve? How would you quantify it?"
- "Can you share with me your plan of action for putting this new web design project in place?"
- "What other options are you considering?"
- "Can you share with me your budget range for this project?"
- "Can you walk me through the decision-making process at your company on a project such as this?"
- "What is your ideal time frame for this project?"
- "What is prompting you to change web design vendors?"

Mitch's team leader took these questions with her to meet with her contact at the client's company.

As she started going through the list of questions, the conversation seemed to go well. The client explained that the company was looking for a web design that would allow customers to order products, post reviews, and suggest innovations. But when the team leader got to the question about why the company had decided to change design vendors, the client danced around it and ended up giving only a superficial response. Still, Mitch's team leader pressed on: "Did something happen with your former vendor that caused you to be unhappy?" Again the client failed to give a concrete answer to the question, leading the team leader to conclude that there had been no problem with the "former" vendor. In fact, the vendor was not "former" at all. The company was simply using Mitch's team to gain a better bargaining position with its current vendor.

The team leader left the meeting dejected and disappointed. She went back to the office and informed Mitch that there would be no big project for their team. Mitch, too, was disappointed, but he was also heartened by the fact that through his smart management, he had limited the amount of time his team had spent on this bid. Further, he knew he had taught his team two valuable lessons: one, about how to manage their time, and, two, to guard against letting enthusiasm about a possible opportunity get in the way of proper preparation.

The next example is another common problem in business. Lisa's team had spent the last several weeks working on a bid for a government contract. But she had been away on vacation when her team initiated this project so it had not been fully vetted. On the day before the presentation of the bid, Lisa called her team together to discuss their strategy. As this was her first real opportunity to take a closer look at the project, she was careful to ask her team to explain the specific needs of the client. The team leader explained that the government agency had contacted him to invite him to make a bid.

At this point, Lisa became apprehensive because she was coming to the realization that her team had not done their homework before committing resources to this project. She decided to contact the government agency herself, to ask important questions about the project. She discovered that in order to fulfill this customer's needs, her team would have to devote themselves 100 percent to the project for the next four months. She knew they could not do this without help because they already had several other customers under contract. Luckily, Lisa still had enough time to hire some of her former interns to take over the routine needs of their current clients during that four-month period Thus, she found a way to satisfy her company's existing clients while at the same time adding a prestigious new client, thereby expanding the reputation of her business.

We're not saying that asking research questions will ensure that you win every client, every time. In any case, as you undoubtedly know, not every client will be right for you and your company.

What we are saying is that conducting due diligence prior to making a commitment will ultimately maximize your time and your team's resources. Not only will this allow you to better serve the clients you currently have, it also will prevent unnecessary risk-taking for your company.

MAINTAINING A STRONG CONNECTION

All too often, once a new contract has been signed, businesspeople will naturally shift their attention to other, more pressing issues. As managers, we tend to focus on things that are going wrong. If we do not hear the customer complaining, we may assume everything is going well, and we are relieved. A word of caution is in order here: Do *not* take your clients for granted. Just because a client is not complaining, or seems satisfied with what you are doing, does not mean there's nothing to be concerned about. It is critical at this juncture to continue to ask the right questions, and provide the right types of services, so that this relationship will last for the long term.

We worked with a client, Tom, whose business was flatlining. To uncover his problem, we spent a few days with him in December. Tom, we learned, wanted to impress Anna, his contact at the firm of one of his larger customers, by making sure he was on time with his deliveries that month. He went out of his way to get her a shipment 20 days before she needed it. Unfortunately, Tom never bothered to ask Anna if this was something that would benefit her. As it turned out, Anna was inconvenienced, and thus annoyed, when the shipment came early, because now she had to find somewhere to store it, and her staff had to keep track of it until they were ready to use it. And because December is one of Anna's busiest months, she was even more stressed than usual by this unexpected early delivery. When Tom called her up the next week to follow up, he was hoping to hear how pleased she was by his initiative. Instead, she chewed him out.

Clearly, Tom did not succeed in strengthening his relationship with Anna. Additionally, he had wasted time making this early delivery, when he could have been doing something much more productive.

How could he have known what his important customer needed? As you can imagine, the answer seemed simple enough to us. All Tom had to do was set aside some time to talk with Anna and ask her questions about her business and how he could be a better service provider. Had he done that, he would have learned that December is Anna's busiest month and, consequently, is probably not the best time to add to her workload. He might also have discovered that she would benefit from split deliveries during busy months to prevent storage problems.

What types of questions should you ask existing clients to more fully understand their business and how you can better help them? First, you need to ferret out any factors that are disrupting your customers' business regimens. If you know your customers' cost and risk factors, you are better positioned to reduce them, and it might mean that clients would be willing to pay more for your products and services to improve their bottom line.

The next list of questions are designed to help you start a dialogue with your existing clients. You may have already asked some of these questions when you first began the relationship, but remember, businesses are constantly evolving, and things can change so drastically and quickly in today's environment that it's essential for you and your team to keep up with the shifting needs and desires of your clients. That way, you can steer them toward any new products or services they might not have needed in the past but do now.

- "Who are some of your current top customers? Are you able to serve them as well as you would like?"
- "What has been the most notable trend among your customers over the past year?"
- "Has your customer base changed over the last year? If so, how?"
- "What is your greatest competitive advantage?"
- "Why do customers buy from you?"
- "What do customers like most about doing business with your company?"

- "What complaints do you hear most often from your customers? What steps are you taking to improve in those areas?"
- "Would you explain to me the differences between your profitable customers and your unprofitable ones?"

Next, you might want to ask questions about your clients' company cultures. Culture encompasses everything from how purchasing decisions are made to the relationships between departments to how changes in the company are proposed and implemented. Questions like the following allow you to be a "fly on the wall," giving you access to a corporation's inner workings. You can then anticipate problems before they arise.

Here are pertinent company culture questions you can ask any existing client:

- "Can you explain to me how your decision-making process has changed since the merger?"
- "Share with me your thoughts on this upcoming project. How does your team feel about it? What about your boss and/or your fellow managers?"
- "How do the departments in your company interact with one another?"
- "What is the turnover rate at your company? How does that affect your profitability when you factor in training and hiring costs?"
- "How would you describe the relationship between your corporate headquarters and your subsidiaries?"

STRENGTHENING THE BOND

Asking questions not only allows you to more fully understand your customer, it also offers you the opportunity to take your relationship to the next level, where you become more of a partner and advisor. The problem, we've found, is that too many managers fail to follow through on this step. Why not? They do not want to "push the envelope." Instead, they hang back and wait for their clients to approach them for more business, or to institute other changes in their relationship status. Another mistake managers make is to work on projects without keeping their clients fully informed as to what they are doing or how hard they are working. This lets potential opportunities slip through their fingers and, worse, raises the risk that another vendor will swoop in and charm their existing clients with new ideas and more attentive service.

If managers wait for their customers to affirm and expand their relationship, chances are they will hear about it only after the customers have taken their business elsewhere. Do not make this mistake! Be proactive—address any problems as they arise, and take advantage of any opportunities by asking these relationship-strengthening questions of your existing clients:

- "What do you feel we are/I am doing right to sustain our business relationship?"
- "What could you and I be doing differently in order to ensure that you achieve your goals?"
- "If you could enhance one thing about our business relationship, what would it be?"
- "How can I make your job a little easier?"
- "Which of your objectives should we be most closely focused on to serve you better?"
- "If someone asked you why you do business with us, what would you say?"
- "In what way(s) are we helping you achieve your goals?"
- "Which goals would you like to see us accomplish for you in the next 12 months?"
- "What would it take on my part to win the business you are currently giving to our competition?"

A question like "How can I make your life easier?" might seem insincere when coming from a stranger, but when asked by a professional colleague who has spent considerable time building a business relationship with you, it will come across as very genuine. Keep this in mind when asking these questions: Not only will you learn what you are doing right, you will also become attuned to any improvements you might be able to make for this client—and possibly for other clients as well. Just as important, these questions also serve the purpose of reminding your clients why you are so valuable to them, giving you and your company a measure of security should an unknown vendor arrive on the scene with the intention of taking your place. Clients will be much less likely to be swayed by, say, the offer of a small decrease in price from one of your competitors if they have just had a conversation with you during which you reminded them of all the advantages you and your company bring them.

Another avenue to pursue when strengthening existing business relationships is to expand your contacts within each of your client organizations. As we learned from the hotel example at the beginning of this chapter, you should never rely on only one or two contacts to perpetuate your relationship. What happens if those individuals change jobs, retire, or get laid off, and there's no one else at the company who has any idea who you are or what you do? Once you have solidified a relationship with one person, it is time to extend your reach to others within the department and then in different departments.

By following our advice so far in this chapter, you will already have gained pertinent information about how decisions are made within the client's company, which departments have the most influence, and the type of customers they attract. Now is the time to use this knowledge to request meetings with others you think might be positioned to take this business relationship to the next level. Here's how:

Imagine you have a contact, Janet, who is a production manager for a large corporation which has been one of your clients for the last 18 months. You are now ready to take this relationship to the next level. Make an appointment with Janet to sit down and discuss how things are going and how your services have helped her and her company for the last year and a half. Assume that, for the most part, your work with this client is going well. Yes, there may have been some issues with the production line, and Janet has asked you several times to rush some shipments and put other orders on hold. This has caused a bit of tension because meeting this request has forced you and your colleagues to disappoint several of your smaller customers.

After discussing and confirming with Janet that she has been satisfied with the client-vendor relationship, ask her some of the following questions in an effort to extend your reach within the corporation:

- "Janet, we are really grateful for the business we have done for you over the past year and a half. As we look to the future, we are evaluating ways to grow your business and eliminate some of the production issues of the past so that we can be sure to give you the best possible service at all times. Going forward, what do you and I need to do differently to ensure a good outcome for both of us?"

- "Which other departments do you think could benefit from meeting with us so that we can streamline your operations?"

- "We would like to improve our turnaround time and eliminate any service glitches. With whom should we speak in order to make those changes?"

- "Has your company ever considered creating a stocking program to rectify the current problems? Who would be the person to initiate such a program?"

Our point is this: If you wait for Janet to introduce you to others in the company, you're probably wasting your time; she has other things on her mind. This is your responsibility; you have to overcome the fear of hearing the word "no" and ask for those introductions. Usually, a satisfied client will be happy to acquaint you with others in his or her organization. By extending your client network in this way, you will be able to blend strategic thinking with solutions to everyday issues. Remember, Janet does not have all of the answers; no one person in a company ever does. By meeting with her counterparts in other divisions, you will gain greater insight into the company at large and, possibly, find ways to expand your services to suit their needs.

If, however, when you ask for introductions to other company contacts, your client appears guarded or elusive, you probably do have cause for worry. Either your relationship is not as strong as you think it is or your contact has less power and influence than you thought.

FIXING WHAT'S BROKEN

Keep in mind that business relationships are constantly evolving. There is always a new challenge to tackle or a new problem to solve. For example, even when sales are through the roof, you should not sit back and rest on your laurels. Your client is thinking, "Sure, this month went great, but how do we keep it up for next month and the month after that?" You want to anticipate these concerns on behalf of your clients, so you can be prepared to offer solutions when they are needed.

The first step, always, is to identify the problem and its source. Is your client upset because you did not do what you said you would, or is something going on in his or her company that is worrisome? If you have caused a problem for your client, the first and most important thing you must do—and quickly—is take responsibility and ask how you can fix the issue to your client's satisfaction. Here are five easy steps to follow when this is the situation:

Step 1: Listen, and do not interrupt—Give your client a chance to explain the problem and to go into as much detail, or vent as much frustration, as needed.

Step 2: Apologize—Do not offer excuses or try to put the blame on someone else. Simply say, "I am sorry this happened."

Step 3: Sympathize—Make sure that your client understands that you realize the importance of this problem.

Step 4: Detail the plan you intend to follow to resolve the issue— Come to this "fix-it" meeting armed with a plan for how you will fix this problem; present your solution and ensure that it will never happen again. Put the plan in writing so your client can see how serious you are about addressing this issue. Make sure to include a time frame for how long the adjustment process will take.

Step 5: Follow up to make sure the problem has been resolved—Do not promise the moon and then fail to deliver it. Go back to your client after the issue has been resolved to discuss how the repair process went and to learn whether or not your client is pleased with the results. If the client still feels the need to vent at this time, or to discuss how and why things went wrong in the first place, repeat step 1—listen, and do not interrupt. That said, do not allow your client to linger over this failure of yours. Remember, it is impossible to completely avoid making errors in business. Just keep in mind that what clients typically remember the longest is not that there was a problem, but what your response to it was. Your goal here is to make the client feel valued and important.

Perception problems are trickier to address than tangible ones. We have all worked hard on a project only to get a tepid response, or none at all, from a boss or client. Frequently, the reason is that others are simply unaware of all that we do. It is up to us, therefore, to help our clients monitor our activities so that they have a thorough understanding of the effort we put in and the results we are producing. Like us, clients have their hands full with their own day-to-day responsibilities, so usually when they do get involved it is when problems arise. That is why clients need to be reminded of the value you are providing when things are going well—and it is up to you to remind them.

As consultants, we know the necessity of demonstrating our value. At the end of our training sessions, we always make a point of celebrating success, making observations, and recommending next steps. We provide our clients with 30-day and 60-day reports to document the effects of our programs. Without these reports, our client companies would have no way of quantifying how much we have helped them. These reports are instrumental in helping us garner repeat business; they also make it easy for our clients to recommend us to others, because they have concrete evidence of what we are capable of accomplishing.

Here is an example of how this works: We spent four months with a West Coast electrical distributor providing training for managers and sales representatives. Following the training sessions, we asked the top-level managers to require each participant to report a success they experienced after using our techniques at 30 days and 60 days out. At the end of the 60 day period, we found more than $6 million of sales could be directly attributed to our training sessions. The company managers were inundated with these success stories and so were able to see firsthand how much value we added to their company. If we had not documented the total revenue directly attributed to our project, the client would not have had undeniable proof about how successful our program had been.

This is why you must ask a client, "What are your goals?" You can then direct the focus of your projects to specifically address those goals, and then document when you help them reach those benchmarks. Finally, one of the smartest things you can do is to write your customers a letter at the end of a project outlining all of the services you provided to them, and close with a heartfelt "thank you" for the opportunity. The next time they want to work with you, they will have concrete evidence to demonstrate why you (and not someone else) should continue to get their business.

For more information on topics discussed in this chapter, visit our website at: www.questionsthatgetresults.com/relationships.

CHAPTER 11

Questions That Manage Your Career

Patricia came to us last year, frustrated and worried about the future of her career. We had met her a few months earlier while doing a consulting project for the company where she worked. She had always been a top performer in the organization, so it was no surprise when she was promoted to account management three years ago, where, as key account manager, she oversees top-tier clients. Other managers often seek her advice because of her unique ability to strategically develop new accounts and then manage them effectively. In fact, she was probably the best salesperson the company had in the region.

In the past, Patricia was on top of the world professionally. She was routinely showered with accolades in her performance reviews and was always given extremely positive feedback by upper management. Then, the week before she asked for our help, two events occurred that left her unsure about where her career was headed, and she sought our guidance as to what her next step should be.

The first event occurred via a phone call she received from a former colleague who had started his own company eight years ago. Jose was doing exceptionally well for himself, and Patricia had wisely kept in contact with him. He called her because he wanted to talk about the possibility of her taking the position of senior vice president of sales and marketing at his company. Jose let her know that her experience, track record, and client relationships would be tremendous assets to his organization. In this new position, she would earn nearly twice her current salary; she also would be given a number of attractive perks, including a company car and membership at an exclusive country club.

Patricia was flattered, of course, and interested to find out more about the position. It would obviously be a big step up from her current job, as Jose had told her that she would play an instrumental role in directing corporate growth and shaping company strategy—things she had little say about at her current company. Patricia was very conflicted, however, because the new job would require her and her family to move from their home in Minneapolis to the company's headquarters in Chicago. Other factors concerned her about this offer, as well: a possibly brutal travel schedule, lots of corporate meetings, and direct responsibility for 40 employees.

The second event was a conversation Patricia had with her boss, Arthur. During her biannual performance review, Patricia had broached the topic of her future at the company. She had been working there for 11 years and during that time had sacrificed a great deal in order to move up the ranks. Many business trips had taken her away from her family for days at a time, and many nights she worked late and did not get home until after her kids had gone to bed. Patricia was now starting to wonder if all of that time spent working had been worth it. That is why, during this performance review (which took place two days after the call from Jose), Patricia said to Arthur, "I am proud to have worked here for 11 years and to have learned so much," followed by the question, "I was wondering what role you see for me in the near future?" Arthur, she noticed, seemed a little bit taken aback by her question. In answering her, he stumbled over his words even as he praised her for the outstanding results she had achieved last year and reminded her how valuable she was to the company. But he seemed to be grasping for something concrete to say. Eventually, he said he would have to think about it and get back to her.

When Patricia called us, we could certainly understand her confusion and concern. She had invested 11 years of her life at a company and now got the impression that her boss either had no clue or did not seem to care what her future there might be. Meanwhile, an opportunity from another company had presented itself that seemed too good to be true. She wanted to know what steps she could take to assure that the decision she made would be the best one for herself and her family.

The first piece of advice we gave Patricia was to step back and take a look at her career and her life as a whole. This is something too many of us fail to do. We change companies, or even industries, when something "better" comes along, without carefully evaluating how those choices might affect us 10, 15, or 20 years down the road. Or we change jobs because of other factors such as geography, family circumstances, the desire to get away from a bad boss, or simply because we want a change of scenery. What we should do instead is to figure out what we really want from our careers and what we have to offer in return as professionals. Therefore, we told Patricia that before she made any decisions, she needed to take time to complete some assessments of her strengths and weaknesses, and to determine what she wanted from her career, going forward.

WHAT DO YOU WANT FROM YOUR CAREER?

In life, it is much easier to be reactive than proactive. Instead of plotting out your goals and then taking the specific, necessary steps to fulfill them, you allow outside forces to guide your actions. If, say, you are offered a promotion or more money, your tendency is to automatically take it without considering the options. Unfortunately, often the result of this approach for people who take it is to wake up one morning and realize that, for example, they hate business travel and yet spend half their waking hours doing it; or they are happiest living in San Diego, but for some reason they have spent the last five years in Chicago. All too often, we hear someone say, "I don't know how I ended up doing what I am doing."

To avoid falling into this trap, the first step is to ask yourself direct questions about what you want out of your career and, ultimately, your life. The answers that you give to these questions will most likely change over time; chances are, what is important to you in your twenties and thirties will not be the same in your forties, fifties, and sixties. Keep this in mind, and come back to these questions as your life and career evolves.

We strongly recommend that you answer these questions on paper (as opposed to in your head), as we've found this garners the best, most honest results for our clients.

- Am I willing to travel for business? If so, what percentage of time am I willing to be away from home—how many nights and/or weekends each month?
- How much time am I willing to spend commuting every day?
- Am I willing to move or relocate? Where would I be willing to go? Where would I not be willing to go?
- How many hours a week am I willing to work? How willing am I to bring work home in the evenings and on weekends?
- How important to me is creativity in making my career fulfilling?
- Do I want more, less, or the same amount of responsibility I have now?
- How much money do I need to make in order to be happy and to meet my financial obligations?
- How important is a learning environment to me?
- How high do I want to climb on the corporate ladder (e.g., assistant vice president, vice president, president, CEO, CFO)?
- What am I willing to give up (money, leisure time, time with family, my current location, status, prestige, seniority, etc.)?
- What am I not willing to give up?
- How important is being independent?
- Am I willing to go back to school for another degree or certification?

- Do I want to start my own business? How important is it that I follow my dreams?

- How important is job security?

- Do I need to work for an established company, or could I be happy working at a start-up?

- How important is recognition? Do I need an impressive title to make me feel successful?

- Do I want to simplify my life by stepping back from my career and focusing on other things?

- At what age do I want to be financially secure enough that I have the option to retire or pursue other opportunities?

- In the future, do I want to retire and stop working altogether, or simply have the freedom to work less?

- Knowing what I know now, what would I do differently in my career to this point? Based on that, what is holding me back from taking action? Is there an immediate step I can take to begin implementing change?

Once you have answered these questions, take some time to reflect on what you've written. In our consulting work, we find that many of our clients realize they have conflicting wants and needs. They might want a high level of recognition and responsibility, yet they also value their leisure time too much to work the long hours it would take to gain that high-ranking position. Or, they want to start their own business but are not willing to give up the security of a guaranteed paycheck. No doubt you, too, will have answers that conflict, so what you then have to do is decide which of your needs and wants are most important. This is something only you can decide.

Take Patricia, for example: She might decide that having a high-paying job with a lot of recognition and responsibility is worth the inconvenience of moving her family to a new city. Or, she may find that she is not willing to move, no matter how tempting the offer. Either way, only Patricia (and her family) can make that decision—she cannot, and should not, expect someone else to make it for her.

WHAT DO YOU HAVE TO OFFER?

Before you make any decisions about your career based on your answers to the questions presented in the previous section, you need to consider other important factors. It is not enough to know what you want out of your career; you also need to be confident in regard to what you have to offer. What are your strengths and weaknesses as a professional, and how will they affect your career path?

The easiest way to explain this is with an exaggerated example. There are millions of kids in the United States who want to grow up to be professional athletes, but there are only a few who are willing to do what it takes to make it to the top. Those few are willing to practice enough, sacrifice time with friends and family, and forgo other opportunities in order to make it as a professional in their chosen sport. But, in the end, even fewer out of that group will be successful each year. Why? Simply, because even though there are many who are willing, only a fraction actually possess the talent and skills needed to go the distance. The same is true in nonathletic professions. Once you have identified your dreams, you need to assess honestly whether those dreams align with your abilities.

More specifically, in order to assess yourself as a professional, you first must be willing to be honest with yourself and, second, to listen to unbridled honesty from others. There are four assessments we recommend that you complete to create the most accurate picture of your skills and abilities. They are:

1. Self-assessment
2. Peer assessment
3. Employee assessment
4. Superior assessment

In the following sections, we break down each type of assessment to explain how to go about attaining the information you need and then how to process it.

1. Self-Assessment

In this assessment, you are trying to uncover your strengths and weaknesses. Everyone faces his or her own unique set of challenges, and the questions that comprise this assessment are designed to help you identify yours. Admittedly, the process can be difficult, but it is vitally important if you want to really know where you stand.

Another important issue to consider here is your self-concept, which is simply the set of beliefs you have about yourself. Commonly, people allow their self-concept to hold them back because they don't believe they can achieve what they want. An example would be a man who thinks he is not smart enough to be a top-level executive. He might have all the skills and qualifications, but he will never position himself to get the job because he lacks confidence that he has what it takes. The only way to alter your self-concept is to first become aware of it and then systematically question your beliefs to determine whether or not they are accurate.

In addition to answering the questions we have provided here, you also should consider completing a personality test such as the Myers-Briggs to find out, for example, whether you are an introvert or extrovert and how that might affect your career choice. The Myers-Briggs test will also help you understand how you make decisions and process information.

You can find other highly reputable self-assessment tools online as well, such as TTI, Kolbe, MAPP, DISC Profile, and Keirsey. Any of these tools can help you measure where your skill level falls among others in your industry. Visit our website, www.questionsthatgetresults .com/assessments, to find more information about these products. Once you have completed one or more of these assessments, you should combine the information from them with your answers to our questions. Again, we strongly recommend that you write out your answers.

Here are the questions to ask yourself:

- Which activities in my current position do I perform well?
- Which activities in my current position do I struggle with?

- Do I have the experience necessary to qualify for a promotion within my current field?
- Am I detail-oriented or do I tend to focus more on the big picture?
- How skillful am I at: public speaking, writing, and persuading? Do I enjoy these activities?
- How effective am I at: budgeting, forecasting, marketing, planning, and administration? Do I enjoy these tasks?
- How adept am I at: meeting new people, dealing with confrontations, navigating corporate bureaucracy and politics, and terminating underperforming employees? Do I enjoy these tasks?
- Am I proficient at developing new business?
- How good am I at handling rejection?
- Do I work well with others, or do I work best on my own?
- Do I enjoy being part of a team?
- Do I want or need to be team leader?
- Which activities do I enjoy in my current position?
- Which activities do I avoid?
- Do I have the talent to coach employees?
- Am I skillful at delegating tasks to others?
- Do I have what it takes to motivate others to work harder?
- How do I express myself best, through verbal or written communication?
- What new skills would I need to develop in order to earn a promotion/accept a new job? How can I go about acquiring those skills?
- What self-limiting beliefs are getting in my way? What can I do to overcome them?
- If there is a specific job I am thinking of pursuing, what are the skills and key activities necessary to succeed at that job? What do others in this position spend their time doing?

This question is really important, because many people think they have an idea of the activities a certain job entails, but are either misinformed or unaware of the true nature of the job. A young friend of ours earned a bachelor's degree in history and education and a master's degree in history, with the intent of teaching history at the high school level. After several years of teaching, she left the profession feeling like a failure. When we asked her what happened, she told us that she had assumed that most of her time would be spent *teaching* students about history; instead, she spent more than 50 percent of her time on disciplining them, doing paperwork, and calling parents. She remarked, "If I had known this is how teachers spend their time, I would have gone to school for something else." If she had spent time beforehand conducting a self-assessment followed by research into her planned profession, she probably would have saved herself years of frustration and anguish.

Remember this question when you are considering switching companies, taking a promotion, or if you are just starting out in the working world. You need to understand the activities associated with a position *before* you take it so that you can accurately determine whether they are activities you enjoy doing and can excel at.

- Which behaviors do I currently exhibit that are beneficial in my current position but might become a hindrance if I were to get a promotion/take a new job? Can I change or develop those behaviors?

This may seem like an odd question, but we have come across this problem more than once. You may recall from Chapter 9, "Questions that Manage Upwards," that we discussed an engineer who had been promoted to a management position. He struggled greatly in his new role because he was so detail-oriented that it took him too long to complete all of the various tasks associated with it. While attention to detail is an asset as an engineer, it can be a flaw when you have to manage a large group of people and are expected to delegate those details to others so that projects can be completed quickly and efficiently.

Once you have completed the self-assessment, we suggest that you write a description of yourself (based on your self-assessment, personality, and industry tests). A hint: Writing it in the third person (i.e., "Patricia is an extrovert who enjoys working with others . . .") may enable you to be a little more objective with your description. Keep this description handy, so you can compare it to what others say about you during the next phase of assessments. Eventually, you will use all of the information you are gathering to make a fully informed decision about the direction your career path will take.

2. Peer Assessment

You may need to brace yourself before you embark on peer evaluations. This type of assessment can be risky because there is the possibility that someone might try to sabotage you so he or she can advance his or her own career. Nevertheless, peer assessments can be enormously helpful, because your peers are, in most cases, best positioned in the company to evaluate your performance, since they do the same job as you.

To make the most of peer assessments, we advise the following: (1) Include those of your peers whom you most admire and trust fully to be completely candid with you. (2) If you hear the same comment more than once (especially if it is negative), consider that it might be true, regardless of your beliefs to the contrary. (3) Take notes on these assessments so that you can more accurately compare them to your self, employee, and superior assessments.

Here are the questions you should ask your peers:

- "I have been thinking about that project of mine that fell apart last week. Can you help me understand what part of that was my fault? What do you think I could have done differently?"
- "I am glad you were able to come with me on that client visit. Can we sit down and assess it? What do you think went well?

What things do you think I could improve upon to make it go better the next time?"

- "I have noticed that you are really successful at meeting your quotas. What do you think I could do to raise my success rate?"
- "I have been thinking about pursuing the position of ___. Do you think I would do well in that type of role?" (Be careful to ask this question only if there is no chance that the person might consider pursuing the same opportunity.)
- "There are five of us on my team; how do you think my performance compares to those of my colleagues?"
- "I am trying to accurately identify my strengths and weaknesses. Could you share with me three things you think I do well and three things I need to work on?"

3. Employee Assessment

You might think you are asking for trouble by giving your employees the chance to evaluate you. Usually, this is not the case, however, because employees have a vested interest in your performance. If there is something you can do to improve the office environment or the efficiency of the team, it is in their best interest to tell you about it. The real problem with most employee assessments is that staff members are understandably reserved about critiquing their managers. That is why it is absolutely essential that you allow them to complete their evaluations anonymously. That is the only way you will get uncensored feedback about your performance. We suggest you go to one of the many online survey sites where you can create an anonymous survey for your employees to fill out. (Visit www.questionsthatgetresults.com/assessments for a list of online survey sites we recommend.)

Here are some questions you might want to include on your employee assessment:

- "How would you describe my role in this organization?"
- "Which functions required for my position do you think I do well?"

- "On which functions do you think I need to improve?"
- "Do you feel you can approach me if you have a problem or concern about your work? Why or why not?"
- "Do you feel you can come to me about a problem with another team member? Why or why not?"
- "Do I provide you with enough good-quality feedback regarding your performance?"
- "How would you describe my communication style?"
- "On a scale of 1 to 5 (1 = poor; 5 = excellent) how would you rate me on the following qualities: organization, communication, flexibility, delegating, coaching, and motivating others?"

4. Superior Assessment

You should already be getting detailed performance reviews from your boss at regular intervals. If you are not, your first step should be to ask your boss for a performance review, one that describes your strengths and weaknesses, how you rate among others in your peer group, and specific advice about how you can improve. If you already have access to these reviews, go back and reread them before you ask any further questions of your boss or others in positions of authority. Once you have a clear idea of how you are perceived by your superiors, you can ask them specific questions about your performance, possibilities for advancement within the company, other areas you might pursue, and any skills you need to strengthen.

Note that some of the questions we provide here are best suited for your direct boss, while others are more applicable to higher-level executives in the company with whom you interact on an occasional basis. This is where networking becomes very important. Ideally, you have been spending time with a variety of the leaders in your company and industry. If you have, now is the time to draw on a multitude of their experiences and opinions in regard to your future. If you have not spent time networking, we advise you to begin doing that immediately.

You should spend time inside and outside of your company making contacts and building relationships with others in your industry. One good way to do that within your own company is to volunteer to work on projects or serve on committees where you will be able to be in direct contact with a variety of top-level executives. You want to have that exposure within the organization so that you become highly visible to those who make decisions about promotions. Outside of your organization, get involved in industry trade groups at the local, regional, and national levels. Offer to serve on boards or committees where you can meet others in your field. Present yourself as a speaker in your area of expertise, and contribute to online discussion groups or blogs in your industry. Yes, all of this will take some time, but we assure you it will be time well invested in your career.

Here are a number of questions to ask your boss and other superiors. Choose only those you are comfortable asking. You may decide to ask relatively general questions or more specific ones (e.g., about new product launches, high-profile projects, or market trends). How you ask the questions, and which questions you choose, depends on whom you are asking. For example, you might ask your direct supervisor out for coffee to discuss your strengths and weaknesses and the areas where you might improve. On the other hand, if you are planning to talk to senior-level executives, your questions should be more strategically oriented and focused on the bigger picture.

The answers you receive should give you valuable insight as to how to position your strengths, improve your network, and share ideas about how you can get more involved in adding value to the organization's success. Remember, it all starts with asking questions like these:

- "You have managed a lot of people in your career. If you could choose just one skill or attribute that you would say is a hallmark of successful people, what would it be?"
- "One of the things that I really enjoy about working here is the opportunity to get involved in a number of different projects. For someone like me, who is interested in ____, on which project would you suggest I volunteer to serve?"

- "What do you see as opportunities for me in this organization over the next three years?"

- "If you were to give one piece of advice to me, considering I currently have the role of ___, what would it be?"

- "From your perspective, what is the one thing that you believe this organization does exceptionally well?"

- "How would you describe our company's unique culture to someone outside the organization?"

- "What are some of the challenges the company needs to prepare for, or avoid?"

- "As you look back on your career here, what has given you the greatest sense of accomplishment and why?"

- "I am interested in finding ways to resolve the issue of _____ in order for the company to achieve more ___. May I share some of my ideas with you? Do you think the company would be open to this type of innovation?"

- "If I wanted to pursue the position of _____ or assume the role of ___, which skills would I need to improve in order to be successful?"

After completing this assessment process, it is time to sit down and compile all the information you have gathered so far. We suggest that you write a document composed of three distinct sections.

- In the first section, you will describe yourself and the things you want to get out of your career (review the first section of this chapter to help with this). This might include: salary requirements, the number of hours you are willing to work, a description of the type of job you want, what you are willing to sacrifice to succeed in the job, and what is of utmost importance to you overall.

- In the second section, you will write a description of your strengths and weaknesses, based on all the assessments you have completed. Next, compare your perception of yourself to how your peers, employees, and superiors evaluated you. This will allow you to gain a more complete picture of both your proficiencies and your shortcomings.

- In the third section, you will write out your goals for the future, for both the short and the long term. Do you want a promotion with more responsibility? Do you want to start your own business? Are you happy where you are, or do you want to change companies and/or industries? Are you hoping to retire, or semi-retire, within the next few years?

Along with your goals, include a step-by-step plan of how you will achieve those goals. In your plan, be sure to include anything you will have to sacrifice, so that you form a true picture of the impact your goals will have on your entire life—not just your career.

WHAT ABOUT PATRICIA?

So what happened to our friend Patricia? First, she decided to do our four assessments so that she could get an idea of what she wanted out of her career and life, as well as her strengths and weaknesses. She found that she did want more responsibility and greater recognition, but that she was very reluctant to relocate her family. Her husband had a good job with the local school district, and her immediate family lived close by, in the suburbs of Minneapolis. Thus, she decided that she would move only if she could not get what she wanted from her current company or another company in the area.

It was difficult for Patricia to be completely honest with herself about her strengths and weaknesses, which led her to rely more on her peer and employee assessments. She learned from them that she was definitely a people person; she was very well liked and thought of as an excellent key account manager. She was, however, seen as a little disorganized and not someone who pays close attention to detail. When we discussed these shortcomings with Patricia, she agreed with them.

As part of her assessment process, Patricia talked with some friends at other companies who held positions similar to the one she had been offered in Chicago. She learned that they spend much of their time traveling, doing paperwork, sitting in on corporate meetings, and discussing planning and budgeting. They also told her they have very little independence and, ironically, less control over their jobs than she did in her current position. She was warned that if she took the new job, she would probably be at the beck and call of her employees, other departments, the executive board, and clients and thus would have very little time to be out in the field. For Patricia, being out in the field, having a lot of freedom, and interacting with clients were three aspects of her current job she liked best. They also happened to be among her strengths.

Patricia also acknowledged that her weaknesses, especially her lack of attention to detail, would be real handicaps if she were to take the senior vice president position. So, she decided that even though the idea of being a senior vice president of sales and marketing was wildly appealing to her, the actual work was not something she would enjoy.

Next, Patricia had to confront her other challenge: to talk with her boss again (and other executives in the company) to determine whether there was a meaningful future for her with her current employer. A few weeks later she broached the topic with her immediate supervisor, Arthur. She was committed to being as honest as possible. She began, "Arthur, I want to talk to you about my performance review a few weeks ago. You had a lot of great things to say about me, but when I asked you where you saw me in the near future at the company, you didn't have an answer. Did you get a chance to think about it and, if so, what did you conclude?" Arthur blinked a few times before answering. "Well, I'm not really sure," he said. "Where do you see yourself?"

Armed with the knowledge she had gained from her assessments and evaluations, Patricia replied, "I know I am an excellent key account manager, but I would like to take on some new challenges. I want to add value to the team and the organization as a whole, and I want to continue my professional growth. I enjoy spending time with clients and my peers, so I know I do not want to sit behind a desk all day. At the same time, I would like to take on more responsibility, earn greater recognition, and be compensated accordingly for my efforts. I see myself taking on a mentoring role for our new hires. We have a fair amount of turn-over, and I think ensuring that new people transition well into their accounts would add value to the organization and help things run more smoothly."

At this, Arthur seemed a little nonplussed at first, but also impressed. Then he began to open up. He shared with her his own struggles to advance within the company. The previous year, he told her, he had been up for a promotion but had been passed over for a younger, more aggressive candidate from outside the company. As a result, Arthur did not have much advice to offer Patricia because he felt stuck in a rut himself. However, he did tell her, "The company is always looking for innovative ways to improve, especially when it comes to the bottom line. If you are willing to suggest something creative like mentoring our new hires, I think the company would be receptive to the idea."

Like a lot of bosses, Arthur no doubt had his own agenda. Clearly, he was not prepared to be much of a mentor or advisor to Patricia, because he was more focused on his own set of challenges. He might, for example, have been thinking, "If she gets promoted, how am I going to replace her? Will she become a threat to my growth or advancement?" Or, he might just have been too worried about any number of other issues to spend time helping Patricia develop her own potential. Whatever the case, Patricia realized she would have to look elsewhere for guidance.

Patricia's next move was to pose her questions to Elizabeth, one of the senior executives she had worked with in the past. She wanted to gain some insight into the future plans of the company, and it was clear that Arthur did not have that type of knowledge. Elizabeth was one of the firm's vice presidents and someone who had encouraged Patricia several times throughout her career. Elizabeth had, in fact, been instrumental in Patricia's promotion three years earlier, and had been impressed with her knowledge of client wants and needs. At the company's annual picnic, Patricia approached Elizabeth with some questions about the general trajectory of the company. After she learned that the company was looking for ways to lower the turnover rate, she broached the topic of a mentoring program with Elizabeth, sharing her thoughts on the issues that might be addressed. She was pleased when Elizabeth encouraged her to put her ideas on paper.

Two weeks later, Patricia and Elizabeth had a more formal meeting to discuss Patricia's ideas. They agreed that this mentoring program would greatly benefit the company; moreover, it would help both of them to achieve a number of their long-term career goals. Subsequently, they worked together on a proposal, which they presented to the executive board later that month.

As a result, Patricia was given a promotion—with the title *National Account Manager*—along with a higher salary. She would be in charge of running the mentoring program, along with taking on other new responsibilities, among them oversight of all the company's high-profile clients, contract negotiations, and strategic business development. The new job gave Patricia the increased recognition and responsibility she sought, but did not entail extra travel or too much time behind a desk.

Ultimately, no one could tell Patricia what to do. She needed to go through a process of self-discovery to find out what she wanted and how and where she could get it. The same is true for you. We cannot give you a prescription for success, because success looks and means something different to everyone. What we can do is provide you with questions you can ask yourself and others to help you find your own success and happiness.

For more information on topics discussed in this chapter, visit our website at: www.questionsthatgetresults.com/yourcareer.

CHAPTER 12

Questions That Assess Opportunities

James has worked in the corporate world for his entire career. He has paid his dues, climbed the ladder, and earned the title of director at an international public relations firm. He is satisfied with his position and is confident he works for a good company and boss. One day, out of the blue, James gets a call from a headhunter. She tells him that another company is interested in talking with him about a position as vice president (a step up from his current role). James would report directly to the president, have significantly greater responsibilities, and receive a 50 percent increase in pay.

Of course, James is flattered by this offer. He is very torn, however, because he has been so happy at his current company. They have treated him well and given him regular promotions. On the other hand, he realizes that his future with them is limited. For the last three years he has consistently received 5 percent raises, and he does not see his earning potential increasing very much more in the future with the company.

This new opportunity has, therefore, piqued his interest, so James agrees to go to the interview. Prior to the meeting, he does some research about the company. He learns that it is well recognized in the industry and growing rapidly. He also discovers that the position he is interviewing for has been held by three different individuals during the last two years. This raises a red flag, but he decides not to jump to any conclusions about what it might mean.

James's first interview is with the director of Human Resources. She asks a lot of questions about his background and his current job responsibilities. She then gives him an overview of the position. James is enthusiastic when he hears about the possibilities for growth and the great compensation package. He asks a few questions about job responsibilities, performance expectations and goals, but she does not have specific answers to those questions (which is not unusual for someone in Human Resources). She does tell James that he will be able to ask his questions of corporate team members during follow up interviews. At the end of the meeting, the director of Human Resources tells James that she is impressed with his experience and track record and that he will be invited back for a second interview.

The positive feedback James received during the first interview understandably pumped up his ego, and he goes into the second meeting feeling really optimistic about this potential new position. During the second interview, he meets with the two top executives at the company. The meeting goes well—once it starts, that is. For although it was scheduled to begin at 9:00 AM, it does not actually take place until 10:30. James is a little put off because during that hour and a half, he was made to wait in a conference room by himself, during which time no one bothered to check on him; he was never offered a cup of coffee or even told the location of the bathroom, should he need it. Still, he chalks this lack of professionalism up to the fact that the company is growing rapidly and the top executives are busy people; besides, he thinks, this is probably one of the reasons they need someone like him to help run things.

When the two executives finally arrive at the conference room, they apologize profusely for making him wait so long. James notes they seem a little disorganized—at first, they cannot even find a copy of James's resume. Once they do, and the conversation finally gets started, it goes well. The execs ask James questions about his strategies for bringing in new business, for handling typical client problems, and for working under pressure. Both seem very pleased with his answers. Again, James does not ask many questions because by the time the executives are done with theirs, it is 1:00 PM. James is famished and desperately needs to use the men's room. As a result, James' attention is diverted from the questions he had planned to ask.

A week later, he gets a call to set up a meeting with the senior vice president of Operations. During that meeting, James becomes a little annoyed, although he hides it well, because this executive constantly interrupts the interview to respond to e-mails on his Blackberry. Still, at the end of the 45-minute meeting, his mood is lifted when the senior vice president tells James that he likes what he hears and wants to introduce him to the president of the company. The meeting with the president is mostly pleasantries and shoptalk. The president tells James that he is always very busy, and rambles on about how he started the company. He then informs James that the key to succeeding in this job is to "hit the ground running." This does not concern James because he considers himself to be self-motivated and prides himself on getting things done.

The following week James gets a call from the director of Human Resources offering him the job. As she runs down the details of the complete compensation and benefits package, James gets really excited. Yes, there are a few things that struck him as "off" about the company—it was a little more chaotic than he is used to, and the personalities of some of the executives appeared to be a little strange—but he wants to move forward in his career and decides that this is his chance to do that. He also concludes he has no concrete reason to turn down the position and thinks how thrilled his family is going to be at the prospect of a significant salary increase.

After only several weeks, the honeymoon is over for James at his new job. He has come to realize this company is more than a little dysfunctional. The management provides almost no guidance to its employees, so they are forced to fly by the seat of their pants. His boss is often away on business trips, and when he is in the office he is a whirlwind of activity. His coworkers are nice enough, but very guarded when it comes to sharing information and ideas. Then, after only five months on the job, James's boss sends him an e-mail late one Friday night to let him know that his position is being eliminated due to "corporate restructuring."

James thinks to himself, "It wasn't a good fit. They are right; but what could I have done differently?" He recalls that he sensed something was "off" during his interviews. He reminds himself how disorganized things seemed and that people were always running around putting out fires. In retrospect, he knows he should have asked some questions about those issues, but he was so flattered by the offer and excited about the higher salary that he did not let himself consider the negatives. If he had taken the time to ask the right questions during the interview process, he could have avoided this disappointing outcome and either waited for a better job to come along or negotiated for better compensation with his previous employer.

WHY CANDIDATES FAIL TO ASK THE IMPORTANT QUESTIONS

Unfortunately, we can recount thousands of stories similar to James's. So many people go into interviews prepared only with general questions to ask of their potential employers, and in this way let the interviewers control much of the discussion. There are a number of reasons why:

- *Fear:* Many candidates do not want to be seen as "rocking the boat," afraid they might give a potential employer the impression that they are prying, or looking for faults. They are afraid to send the wrong signal for fear they will not be considered for the job.

- *Greed:* Often, job candidates are so thrilled by the opportunity and possibilities of a new position that they do not think to ask about the details of the job. They hear the title or the high annual dollar figure and they are sold without making sure that there are no negatives being overlooked.

- *Pride:* Even if their gut tells them that something about a job or company is not right, many people will override their instincts because they are so excited to be offered the job. Especially if they really need the job or are being flattered by a potential employer. Many candidates will push aside any negative impressions and let their pride or enthusiasm silence their common sense.

- *Denial:* Often, candidates will pick up on problems at a potential new company but will convince themselves that they are so good at what they do that they will be able to rise above such issues. If, for example, they hear that others have had problems with the position or the boss, they will talk themselves into believing they can do it better.

ASKING THE RIGHT QUESTIONS DURING A JOB INTERVIEW

Too many candidates go into an interview thinking that the interviewer is in control and holds all the cards. On the contrary, we know from experience that many interviewers are disorganized, unprepared, distracted, and just going through the motions. When they ask the question, "Can you tell me a little bit about yourself?" they often don't really pay attention to the answer. To you, the candidate, this means that in order to determine with any degree of certainty that this is a good opportunity, you need to bring balance to the interview by making it more interactive. You need to be fully engaged and ready to ask pertinent questions in order to get as much information as you can to help you make an informed decision.

You may already know that most people enjoy being asked about themselves and their experiences. So start there, and once you have established rapport with an interviewer, begin to pose questions about the company culture, the possible drawbacks of the position, the personalities of those with whom you would be working, the benefits of joining the company, and the decision-making process of the department. Keep in mind that most management positions require at least two or more interviews, so do not feel compelled to ask all of these questions at the first meeting.

The remainder of this chapter is composed of 10 categories of questions that we recommend you address during an interview. Naturally, some will apply more than others to your particular situation. Do not be afraid to ask these questions, even if the prospect of doing so is intimidating to you. The time to ask the hard questions is now, before you invest your time and energy in a job that is not really right for you.

1. Questions about the Corporate Culture

An often-overlooked topic during the job interview process is corporate culture. Prior to accepting a job, you want to know if you will be a good fit within the organization as a whole. Specifically, you need to find out whether the politics, values, and dynamics of the firm suit you. For example, let's say you are coming from a Fortune 500 company with a very structured environment, one that favors highly systematic processes for new initiatives: How will you feel running a small, entrepreneurial firm where there are no clearly-defined job responsibilities, and decisions are made on the fly?

There are companies whose environments are fun, creative, and spontaneous. Others are more team-oriented; still others are extremely competitive. Further complications may arise if you are considering joining a family-run business. In short, you want to know what you are walking into *before* you take a new job. To help you unearth that crucial information, review these questions you might want to ask to determine the culture of a company:

- "How might the typical employee describe what they love most about working here?"
- "How would you describe the company culture in five words or less? How do you think the typical customer would describe it?"
- "Who else can I talk to in order to learn more about how the company operates?"

- "How does the company celebrate success?"
- "How are changes in policies initiated at this organization?"
- "Every company has its unique issues to contend with; what is the one area that others in this organization might say makes it challenging to work here?"

As you ask these questions, pay attention to key words and phrases you hear and then follow up with questions, if necessary, to clarify responses. For example, "fast-paced" can mean "exciting," but it can also mean "chaotic."

Once during an interview, Paul asked the interviewer what was the most common frustration of the company's employees. The interviewer responded, "Sometimes things do not get done as quickly as we would like." Paul then asked, "What do you mean?" He was told, "Well, for example, we had a new manager come onboard last year and he was not able to get a computer for seven weeks." Paul raised his eyebrows and dug further: "So how do employees deal with situations like that, when it can take longer to get an issue resolved than expected?" The interviewer looked at him, and with a gleam in her eye said, "Patience is key." This exchange let Paul know that while the company seemed like a creative and interesting place to work, it would probably be frustrating for someone like Paul who was used to working in an environment focused on accountability and results.

2. Questions about Who Else Is Involved

You may make a great impression on the interviewer, but that does not mean you will get the job. The decision-making process varies greatly from company to company, and it is your task to find out how the hiring choice will be made. Who makes the final decision? Who has influence on that person? What are the potential roadblocks that could hinder your advancement? These are the questions you want to find answers to during your interviews.

The questions you ask in this category will help you to determine how to better direct this process so you can meet the needs of not just the interviewer but also the requirements (often conflicting) of all those involved. Here are some example questions to consider:

- "Can you walk me through the decision-making process you will follow in choosing the ideal candidate?"
- "What are the steps your organization will take in the selection process?"
- "Who, in addition to yourself, will have an influence on the hiring decision?"
- "Which departments are involved in the hiring process?"

As the interviewer answers your questions, listen carefully for important words and phrases. If, for example, the interviewer mentions another team member repeatedly, it is perfectly acceptable for you to ask to meet with that person—even if it is just to say hello. On the other hand, if the interviewer does not seem to know when or how the hiring decision will be made, it is unlikely that he or she has very much say in the process. Also, if the interviewer is very guarded about sharing information, this should be a cause of concern for you.

3. Questions about the Company's History and Future

In business, as in life, the past is often a window into the future. If you can learn the history of the company and understand how it has evolved over the years, it may give you a preview of what is to come. Questions that enable you to gather information about clients (former and current), as well as how the company has positioned itself in the marketplace, will give you an understanding of what makes the organization tick. Asking a few questions about the past will invariably lead to information about who the main decision makers are in the company—who, often, are not the names listed on the organizational chart. For example, a company's president may be more of a figurehead, and the actual person in charge might be the "retired" CEO, who started the business 50 years ago. Or you might think you are joining a family business, only to discover, after asking pertinent questions, that the family has sold most of its interests, and the company is now run by a corporate board located in another city.

As you can see, it's important to ask questions about the company's history, in order to more fully comprehend what your role truly will be in the organization. The sample questions we give you in this category are, necessarily, broad; you most likely will need to tailor them to your particular situation.

- "You mentioned that you have been with the organization for over 10 years. Tell me, what has been your greatest accomplishment for this company?"
- "So many organizations are trying to differentiate themselves in this commoditized market; what would you say is the one key quality that separates this organization from its competitors?"
- "Can you share with me the history of the position I'm interviewing for? How has it evolved over the years? How has it contributed to the success of this organization?"
- "Every organization has to deal with change; what is the one shift this company is attempting to implement now in order to succeed in the future?"
- "What steps will the organization take to achieve its goals in the next three years?"

No company is going to be without its unique challenges. Your goal is not to try to find the perfect company—in any case, it doesn't exist—but to identify the most pressing issues you most likely will have to deal with if you are offered, and decide to accept, the position.

4. Questions about Your Supervisor

Everyone has a boss; even the president of a company has to report to a board or account to stockholders. That is why, prior to accepting any position, you should find out as much as you can about your boss. This includes learning about his or her goals, objectives, motivations, and personality style, as well as what he or she will expect of you. Examples of questions in this category include:

- "Can you share with me the ideal qualities you are looking for in a candidate for this position?"
- "Based on the candidates you have interviewed so far, which attributes have surfaced as being the most important to you in choosing the right person?"
- "What goals do you have for this position in the short term? What about "the long term?"
- "How do you like to communicate with those who report to you?"
- "What are your professional plans for the future?"
- "Can you walk me through the key areas of responsibility that the person you choose will have to manage?"
- "How will you measure success?"

5. Questions about the Management Team

It is not enough to become informed about the company and the individual you will be reporting *to*; you also need to find out about the people you will be working *with* every day. What personalities will you have to deal with as you strive for success? Have others struggled to work with this team in the past? In what ways do they compete for attention, resources, or budget dollars?

Here are some questions you can ask to learn more about your future coworkers:

- "Can you describe to me how the department heads work together?"
- "How are conflicts among team members resolved?"
- "How long have these managers been working together as a team?"

- "On this team, how are tasks assigned? How are their outcomes evaluated?"
- "How are members of the team recognized and rewarded for their performance?"

If you are told that team members have all been with the company for more than 10 years, and that tasks are assigned based solely on seniority, think carefully about joining the company, for it could mean that it would be very difficult for you, as the newcomer, to gain any traction. You might, as a matter of course, be assigned the least desirable tasks, and thus never—or not for some time—get the opportunity to grow as a leader. On the flipside, it should also raise a red flag if you learn that all of the team members have been replaced recently, and that no one is really sure of who has seniority or how decisions are made.

6. Questions about the Employees You Will Manage

As a manager, you are only as good as your employees. Many managers make the mistake of neglecting to ask critical questions about potential employees and, as a result, end up not having the personnel they need to get their job done. You do not want to end up with incompetent or unmotivated employees working for you—especially if you do not have the power to replace them. Asking a few questions, such as the ones listed here, about those who will report to you will open your eyes to the realities of any new management opportunity.

- "Can you describe to me, one by one, the employees in this department who would report to me, including their strengths and weaknesses?"
- "Who will be my 'go-to guy,' the person I can count on to get the job done every time? Who will be my greatest challenge to manage?"
- "Help me better understand the scope of my authority in this position. Will I have the authority, for example, to replace an individual who is not meeting performance expectations?"
- "How much budgetary discretion will I have in this position?"

- "What did the employees like and respect about my predecessor? What did they dislike about him or her?"
- "What is the history of this department? Has it been successful, or has it struggled?"
- "Can you provide me with job descriptions for those who will report to me?"
- "Who on the staff is achieving their objectives, and who is not?"
- "What are the consequences to those employees who fail to meet their objectives?"
- "May I meet with those who will be reporting to me before I accept your offer?"

We cannot overstate the importance of gathering information about the employees who will be reporting to you *before* you accept an offer. You want to avoid taking a job then finding out that the employees you have been assigned to manage are failing to meet their objectives, and you are not empowered to replace them, withhold salary increases, or take corrective action to turn things around. It works the other way, too. You can be much more confident about accepting a position if you have uncovered information that indicates your future employees are hard workers and excel at their jobs. Remember, you are not just looking for reasons to say "no." It is just as important to find reasons to say "yes" when a great opportunity comes along.

7. Questions to Ask Yourself

These are questions you should ask *yourself*, to determine if you really want to pursue this position and/or accept the job—assuming an offer is made. We strongly recommend that you ask yourself these questions *before* you get an offer, so you will not accept it just because you are flattered by an invitation to work somewhere, even if it is clearly not a good fit for you.

- What will I be able to do in this job that I have not been able to undertake in my current job?

- Are there ways to revamp my current job/role to make me happier, or make it more rewarding?

- Have I attempted to have any discussions with my boss and/or senior management to explore other opportunities at my current organization before I consider taking this new opportunity? If I have not, what's holding me back?

- What qualities or attributes of a position would truly make me content?

- What aspects of this new opportunity cause me concern?

- Who on the team appears to be someone that will be a strong ally and/or will reinforce my personal strengths?

- Does my immediate supervisor appear to be an individual I can turn to for guidance and direction?

- What strengths do I possess that will ensure my success in the job?

- What skills must I develop or improve, and what knowledge do I need to gain, to ensure my success?

- Who on my team might be a threat, or cause me grief?

- What information or feedback have I gathered that is conflicting or confusing?

- From a logical perspective, what would motivate me to accept this job (e.g., salary, benefits, location, career advancement, greater job security)?

- Do I really want this job, or do I feel as though I have to take it? If it is the latter, am I willing to put up with the potential problems that are likely to occur?

- What is the opportunity cost of taking this job? What other opportunities might I be giving up in order to accept this position?

- From a more personal perspective, what would motivate me to take this job (e.g., prestige, recognition, security, freedom)?

Only you can know the "right" answers to these questions. Giving yourself permission to go through this process and determine whether or not a position is a good "fit" will give you the information and perspective you would not otherwise have if you simply made a decision based on your "gut" feeling.

8. Questions about Salary and Benefits

Salary, as we all know, can be a touchy subject, especially if it is brought up too early in an interview. Too many interviewers ask, "How much money did you make last year?" as one of their first questions. It is an offensive question to ask someone at the beginning of a conversation and sets a negative tone for the entire interaction.

Typically when you are asked this question early on, the intent is to disqualify you immediately so that the interviewer can cut the meeting short. If your answer is higher than the salary the company intended to offer, the interviewer will assume you are overqualified and therefore will not be interested. If your answer is significantly lower than the salary range, the interviewer will think, "Great! I can offer a lot less than I was prepared to for this position." Or "There might be something potentially wrong with you since you are earning a lot less than what I am willing to offer." Either way, there is no advantage to you answering this question so early in the interview process. If, however, you are put in this position, we advise you to respond with a question of your own, such as: "Well, since you raised that question, let me ask you, what is the salary range for this position?"

When someone pries too quickly and directly about personal matters in *any* conversation, you can take back control by answering a question with a question. Otherwise, you will usually lose ground by revealing such personal information too early on. That said, if you are uncomfortable taking this approach and feel you must respond, then do so, but be prepared to follow up with a question of your own. Never feel that the interview must be one-sided; remember, it is an exploratory conversation for *both* parties.

Here are a number of ways to ask about salary and compensation:

- "Last year, I earned $X. Now let me ask you: What is the salary range for this position?"
- "How is the compensation package determined?"

- "I was hoping we could discuss my credentials and how I could add value to this organization before we get into the compensation topic this early in the interview. But since you brought it up, what is the salary range for this position?"
- "To what extent is the salary negotiable?"

If you are told the salary is not negotiable, you need to ask about other benefits. Here are some questions when this is the case:

- "Since, as you've told me, the salary is fixed, what are some other areas we can explore to compensate me for what I'll be contributing to this organization?"
- "Are stock options available to managers at this level in the organization?"

Patrick remembers a time when he accepted a job offer because everything seemed perfect. The only topic he and the interviewer had not addressed in detail during the interview was the bonus structure. Patrick had asked some questions about the details of the bonus system, but could not get a straight answer. Instead he was told, "Don't worry about it. We'll take care of you." Patrick had hit it off with this person, and trusted that he was a man of his word. In hindsight, his failure to nail down bonus details turned out to be a huge red flag.

After a year at the company, Patrick was given his 12-month review. During that period, he had brought in more than 50 percent over projections in new business on top of maintaining the existing client list. Understandably, he expected to be compensated commensurately. His boss did give him accolades for a job well done, followed by a few suggestions about areas he could improve on. But when Patrick brought up the issue of a bonus, his manager said, "Well, it has been a tough year for us, and we want to reward you for your efforts, but we just cannot give any bonuses this year." His boss then apologized and added, "Things should go better next year. We will take care of you." This time, Patrick pressed for specifics, but was told by his boss that he'd have to talk it over with *his* boss and the executive committee.

Patrick now realized that his boss did not have the power to give him a bonus, and so after hearing back from his boss that the executive committee would not agree to set a bonus structure, he immediately decided to update his resume and look for a different job.

9. Questions about Accepting a New Position with Your Current Employer

Ironically, managers who would never think of accepting a new job without thoroughly investigating the opportunity first will often make the mistake of jumping at a promotion within their own company without first asking the right questions. Companies know that their employees are flattered by the offer of promotions and title changes. Some depend on the fact that staff members will often move into a new position without realizing what the implications might be.

Do not fall into this trap; make sure first to ask the kind of questions that will give you all you need to know about *any* new position prior to accepting it. Here are some we specifically formulated to guide you in the decision-making process when you have been offered a new opportunity with your current employer. Be sure to also consult the other sections of this chapter to cover all of the bases before you move forward.

- "What are the major responsibilities of this position?"
- "Who will I be overseeing?"
- "What is the salary, bonus structure, and other compensation for this position?"
- "If I take this position now, but an agreement on a new compensation plan has not been finalized, when can we set a deadline to agree to one?"
- "Who will I report to if I take this position?"
- "What is the next step for me if I decide to take on these new responsibilities?"
- "Will I have an assistant or other staff member who will be assigned to work directly for me?"

- "What will my budgetary discretion be in this new position?"
- "To what extent will I be able to make hiring and firing decisions?"
- "What level of decision-making authority will I have in this position?"
- "My plans for the future include a goal to take on greater responsibilities and/or assume the role of _____ within this company. How do you see this new position putting me on that path?"
- "What are the performance expectations for this position?"

One of the mistakes managers make is failing to lay out their desired career path. Instead, many take whatever is handed to them without thinking about how it will affect their future prospects. To avoid this mistake, you must figure out precisely what you want your career to do for you and then make sure you pursue only those opportunities that will further those goals.

10. Questions about Noncompete and Severance Agreements

There is a great deal of turnover at the corporate senior executive level, so it should come as no surprise that companies want to do whatever it takes to prevent their executive talent from being poached by competitors. It is a primary reason so many corporations require their employees to sign noncompete agreements along with their employment contracts.

We know a talented executive named Marie who was hired as vice president of marketing for a big-box store. Only nine months later, due to internal political power struggles, Marie was out of a job. The company gave her a six-month severance package and career placement assistance. Marie, fortunately, had developed a good network in her industry and was able to land another, comparable position within two months. Unfortunately, she had signed a noncompete agreement with her former company, which prohibited her from accepting a comparable position in the same industry for two years. Through the grapevine, her previous employer found out about her new position and threatened to sue if she did not quit. Her new employer, not wanting to get involved in a legal dispute, asked her to resign her new position. Marie could have avoided this problem if she had been more careful during the hiring process at the big-box retailer.

Asking the right questions about severance and noncompete agreements is never easy; it is akin to asking your future spouse to sign a prenuptial agreement. In fact, it is best not to bring up the issue of noncompete clauses at all, if you can avoid doing so. However, if you *are* asked to sign one, be prepared to ask this question:

- "What type of severance package will I be offered should the organization decide to end my contract early? How will I be compensated for the time during which my noncompete clause remains in effect?"

If a potential employer wants you to sign a noncompete agreement but refuses to compensate you for its duration, think very carefully before accepting an offer of employment.

CONCLUSION

The interview establishes the basis of a working relationship between you, your boss, and your new company. It is the time to define roles, to gather as much information as possible, and to lay the groundwork for a healthy give-and-take in the future. Asking the questions provided in this chapter will allow you to demonstrate that you are a strong, capable candidate, one who takes an active role in shaping his or her employment structure. These questions will also serve to guide you as you go through the difficult process of making an informed decision about whether or not to accept the new opportunity. These decisions are too important to make based on "gut" instincts; they need to be grounded in concrete facts and reliable information.

For more information on topics discussed in this chapter, visit our website at: www.questionsthatgetresults.com/opportunities.

CHAPTER 13

Questions That Manage Your Relationships with Your Kids

In many cases when we have worked with business owners and high-powered successful executives, many of them are confident they are in control of their careers and business lives. Their family lives, however, are a different story. At home, they can't claim the same outstanding success or balance. One client confided to us that his family life was a shambles: "My wife sometimes says she thinks she married the company instead of me. With my hectic schedule, it feels more and more like we're two strangers sharing a house. I'm away on business so much; my little boy hardly knows me—I even had to miss his fourth birthday party last week because I had fires to put out at work!"

Often, successful professionals who work hard and put innumerable hours into their careers and businesses will profess: "I'm doing this for my family." That's only partially true. They do, of course, work hard to support their families and keep them fed, clothed, safe and secure. The rest of the truth is that these executives are doing it for themselves, as well. For they have powerful personal drives, egos, and competitive natures. They've also achieved a level of success in their business lives that's very hard to replicate in their personal lives.

It may surprise you to realize why this is so for many of us: We simply don't have the kind of control at home that we do at work. That is, we can control, influence, and motivate people on the job, but back home, trying to reason with a child, teenager, or college-age young adult can leave us so frazzled and frustrated that we often yearn to go back to the office. In short, the stresses of family life can make the work environment seem more welcoming by comparison. At least at the office, we're important; people look up to us. At home, in contrast, we may feel as if we don't get the same respect or attention. We end up feeling more comfortable, more in our element, at the office than we do at home. How did things reach this point? For many, it begins because we spend more of our waking hours in the position of manager than we do as parent. We might begin to feel that we are professionals in the office, but only amateurs at home. When conflict arises with our children, this leads to us shying away from our family responsibilities because they are more complicated and emotionally charged than our professional responsibilities. It does not have to be this way.

When handled well, family time creates a better balance between work life and home life. The key is to make sure that family time is *quality* family time. For example, Paul has a good friend who lives in Southern California. He's the father of two teenagers, a boy and a girl. To spend time with his son, he bought them both dirt bikes, so they could go riding together. But here's what actually takes place: On Saturday mornings, the two of them go into the desert together. But then the son takes off on his dirt bike while the father takes out his laptop computer to catch up on paperwork. Later, on Saturday afternoons, Dad takes his daughter to the mall, where he parks himself on a bench near the food court while she shops or meets up with her friends.

Is the time this father spends with his teenagers quality family time? No. Family time is supposed to involve family members talking and interacting with each other, not merely occupying the same space and breathing the same air.

Here's another example of family time, absent the quality. We have all been in restaurants when a mother or father comes in with one or more children. Instead of the parent using that opportunity to interact with his or her children, the parent spends much of the meal on a cell phone or other technological device while the children either talk to each other, or use their own phones to text friends. These parents are missing out on a huge opportunity to open the doors of communication with their children. They are also sending the signal to their children that they are not interested in what they have to say.

Since the 1960s, people have been talking about a "generation gap." We are not convinced that the problem stems from a generation gap; rather, we think the real problem is a communication gap. This gap causes many family problems that could easily be avoided.

For instance, we know a businessman named Luke who was going through a painful divorce. He was not only mourning the loss of his marriage, but also the separation from his eight year old daughter Samantha. Rather than resign himself to being a weekend parent, he decided to take action. One night he called Samantha and asked her if she wanted to have lunch with him that Friday. She said she would like that very much but that she was in school on Friday. Luke called the school and arranged to pick her up during her lunch hour, promising to return her in time for her afternoon classes. Luke's purpose in scheduling this luncheon was to build a bond between him and his daughter. As a result, he learned to ask questions and listen to what Samantha had to say. They talked about everything: the divorce, her friends, his work, and what she was studying at school.

For the next ten years, until she graduated from high school, Luke made a concerted effort to eat lunch with Samantha on Fridays. Sometimes this meant that he had to bow out of a business meeting, or forgo some travel for work. Luke made all of this effort because he wanted to have a great relationship with his daughter, and he knew he had to work hard to achieve it. Just like all of his professional accomplishments, this personal relationship was worth putting in the time in order to get the results he wanted.

It is easy to tune out as a parent, especially as your children get older and the signs that they need you are less obvious. If you want a good relationship with your children, however, you need to put in as much effort as you do with your professional relationships. If your child says to you, "You don't understand me!" or "You don't know what it is like," what he or she is really trying to tell you is that there is a communication gap. Now, it is true that some of the problems our children face today are vastly different from the ones we faced at their age. Technology has altered the way children interact with each other and the world around them. The answer, however, is not to give up and assume you cannot know what they are going through. You need to step up and engage them, ask them questions to uncover what is happening in their lives.

Before we get to the questions that can help open the doors of communication with your children, we want to share with you several questions that typically *won't* get kids to open up and tell you what's going on, or what they are thinking or feeling:

Question: "How was your day?"
Answer: "Good."

Question: "What did you learn at school today?"
Answer: "I don't know."

Question: "Did you have fun today?"
Answer: "Yes."

Follow-up Question: "What did you do that was so much fun?"

Answer: "I don't know."

Question: "What's going on?"
Answer: "Nothing."

This is kind of like pulling teeth, isn't it? Even when you sense that something is really bothering your child, he or she often will say "no" or "nothing" when you ask them questions like "What's wrong?" or "Are you having a problem?"

The issue with these questions and others like them is that they're too general and will, therefore, get you little more than a lackluster one- or two-word response. The best way to open the lines of communication with children is to begin with the right atmosphere. When children are very young, the milk-and-cookies routine works well to set the right tone for a chat. As kids grow older, sharing a snack can continue to be used to create the type of atmosphere you want. The important thing is to begin in a positive way. Doing activities that they enjoy together like watching a movie, or engaging in an impromptu bit of fun. Throwing a ball around the yard, can create the kind of casual ambience you want. You might also volunteer to help your kids with their chores. Your child will feel like you are helping to make life easier for him or her, while also creating an atmosphere of open communication.

Understanding your children and how they communicate is critically important. And one size doesn't fit all—everybody's different. Whenever Paul's oldest daughter walks in the door from school, Paul and his wife need only to ask her an open-ended question or two and she will start talking. In contrast, his youngest daughter will generally open up only after about 15 minutes of small talk, and sometimes she will remain tightlipped about a problem for much longer—until she feels ready to share with her parents.

As children get older, you often have to change your tactics as well. Teenagers, for example, will feel freer to divulge what they're thinking and feeling when they are confident they are being treated with respect, that their parents won't overreact or impose on them their values or judgment. That is why, when you ask questions of teenagers, be careful how you react, as your responses will mean the difference between opening communications and building barriers that will keep you from knowing what is really going on with your teen.

In order to get your teenager to open up, we suggest following a three-step process:

First, ask a specific question in an area you know is relevant to him or her. It could be about sports, fashion, a celebrity he or she likes, or a social event that took place recently. Examples might be, "Which teams do you think are going to the Super Bowl this year?" Or, "Do you think that the new movie with Miley Cyrus will be good?"

If your teen responds positively, you can try some more probing questions, such as: "Since we are talking about sports, how has baseball practice been going?" Or, "It is crazy to think that just a few years ago Miley was on the Disney channel and now she is in romantic movies. Does that seem strange to you?"

The third step is to continue asking casual questions. You might dig deeper into the original topic, or branch out to other issues—for example, about your teen's friends: "How is Natalie? Wasn't she having a fight with her mom?" Let's say your teen responds, "Yeah, Natalie is having some problems." To which you might reply, "I'm sorry to hear that. What kinds of problems is she having?"

Remember, your replies should convey casual interest or concern, not reveal intense alarm. If your teen detects even the slightest note of overreaction or negativity from you (e.g., "Problem?! What problem?"), it is virtually guaranteed that he or she will clam up.

These types of questions will help you delve deeper into what's on your teen's mind. They might even help teens clarify their values and get in touch with their own feelings, thereby opening the door to more frank discussions between you and your child. Remember: Pause and think before you respond, and show plenty of empathy. How you listen to teenagers depends on the situation, too. For general discussions, when you're trying to get them to open up, it can help to do some enjoyable activity together, like taking a walk or playing a board game.

When you're broaching more serious topics about which teens have deeper concerns or problems, it's important to stop what you're doing, make eye contact, and give them your full attention. Keep in mind that as much as you may want to jump in and immediately pepper your teens with advice, you're better off waiting as long as you can to do so. First, concentrate on finding out more about their thoughts and feelings; go as deep as you can.

Eight Steps for Listening to a Child or Teenager

1. Stop what you're doing.
2. Focus and look at the child—in the eyes, if possible.
3. Ask additional questions that make no assumptions.
4. Withhold judgment and your opinion.
5. Seek to understand.
6. Respond with empathy. It's acceptable to act happy, excited, or even sad; just avoid anger or even mild irritation.

7. If you have a strong reaction, don't show it; instead, use a delaying tactic, by saying something like, "Let me think about it for awhile."

8. Come back with more questions.

It's important to teach our children to take ownership of a problem. When the problem is one of behavior, it's essential to build the child's self-esteem without minimizing the consequences of the undesirable behavior. If your child misbehaves to the point of being disruptive or destructive in any way, it's important to practice what's commonly known as "stand-up parenting," in which parents take a firm stand, setting the standard of behavior for their children by stating early and unequivocally what the consequences will be for bad behavior. This leaves no doubt in children's minds that their parents mean exactly what they say and must be taken seriously.

As an example, Paul's daughter Brooke had a tendency to get distracted in class and chat with her friends while the teacher was talking. The teacher brought this issue to Paul's attention, after which he and his wife sat down with Brooke and explained to her the need to pay attention, not be disruptive, and be more attentive and cooperative in class. She gave then her word she would correct her behavior in the future. Nevertheless, her teacher had to reach out to them again to report two more incidents that occurred later. Here's how they handled it:

Brooke was excited about a school dance coming up—her first one—which she had planned to go to with her friends. But Paul and his wife told her she wouldn't be going because of her continued disruptive behavior in class. That set her off, as you can imagine; she started crying and pleaded with them to give her one more chance. It wasn't easy, but Paul and his wife knew they had to stand by the limits they had set.

The following week, just a few days before the dance, she was like a new child; so pleasant to be around. In the past, her parents had to nag her to do her weekly chores. Not this week; she was Ms. Initiative. She took out the trash, helped prepare the family dinners, washed the dishes, and walked the dog. Paul and his wife were delighted to see this remarkable change in Brooke. Not surprisingly, she approached them the day before the dance and reminded them how helpful she had been all week. She told Paul and his wife that she felt she deserved to go to the dance. Paul and his wife praised her, but reiterated that she would not be going to the dance because she had been repeatedly disruptive in school.

It wasn't easy to be tough with Brooke—of course Paul and his wife wanted to see their daughter experience the thrill of going to her first dance at school, but they stood firm. Make no mistake, punishing their daughter in this way made Paul and his wife miserable. But if they had caved in, the whole exercise would have been futile—a total waste of time and energy. If they had let Brooke go to the dance in the end, it would have taught her that when she got in trouble she could squirm out of it by acting sorry and trying to manipulate her parents and her teacher. Instead, she learned not only that her parents would take corrective action whenever she willfully misbehaved, but also that she had to make sure things never reached that point, because when Mom and Dad lay down the rules, they won't back down. Their daughter had to learn her lesson the hard way, but it was worth it for all concerned. Since this incident, she has been much better behaved at school and at home.

It is also important to avoid lecturing your children or dominating conversations with them. Lecturing or talking over your kids' heads virtually guarantees that they'll tune you out completely. All children, especially tweens and teens, want to be talked *to*, not talked *at*. Make your points clearly and succinctly; stop short of pontificating; and after you've made your point, be willing to listen to what your children have to say.

Don't let yourself get caught up in a power struggle with your children, either. All parents want their kids to understand the importance of what we're saying; and of course we want to listen to their concerns. But if you find yourself arguing with your child, or defending what you're saying, you've become trapped in a power struggle, which nobody will win. The only result will be bad feelings on the part of everyone concerned. Instead, do your best to figure out the main message your children are trying to express—what they're upset about. Let them talk about their feelings so that you can learn what's really at the heart of the problem. Don't waste time and energy arguing or defending yourself; and at all times, be willing to listen.

When behavior issues rear their ugly heads with your children, we suggest asking these questions:

- "What did you do?" (Ask this in a calm, conversational way. If your child doesn't answer, repeat it firmly until they "fess up.")
- "What are the consequences of that type of behavior?" (e.g., "We talked about the iPod being a privilege, and we agreed that if this happened again, we would take it away for two days . . .") Or: "What is the impact on others when you do that?"
- "What do you suggest I do about it?"

This process achieves three positive results. First, it teaches a sense of responsibility, as well as how to actually *take* responsibility. Second, it teaches kids that their actions have consequences. Third, kids learn to become part of the solution, so that you are not seen as the bad guy.

As noted earlier, to maintain openness in these situations, it's important to withhold judgment. Few postures will make kids (and adults, for that matter) shut up and shut down faster than a judgmental look or remark or a shocked expression.

Another reminder: Before you react, use a delaying tactic, such as asking for time to think about the situation. At all costs, avoid saying something you cannot take back and/or might regret.

The earlier you begin working on opening the lines of communication with your children, the easier it will be as they mature. That said, it's never too late to begin! You will be rewarded in lifelong benefits. With awareness and insight, we, as working parents, can be just as effective and successful managing our family lives as we are our professional lives. Asking the right questions, communicating openly, and having a positive attitude will help to make that happen.

For more information on topics discussed in this chapter, visit our website at: www.questionsthatgetresults.com/kids.

Acknowledgments

I would like to thank the following individuals for making this book possible:

The John Wiley Team including Shannon Vargo, Beth Zipko, and Susan Moran.

Jerry Acuff who introduced me to Wiley.

Dave Byers, PBR's marketing, web-designer, and creative genius. Your questions make me think.

Dorian Tenore-Bartilucci, PBR's talented PR expert who has crafted many of my ideas into a work of art.

Karianne Earner-Sparks, a gifted writer and an incredible project manager who questioned our questions. Thank you for sharing your many talents to help us create what we believe will be another best seller just like the last book, *Questions that Sell,* on which you also did a terrific job.

Patrick Connor, my friend and mentor. You always give me great ideas to the questions I ask.

Mom and Dad for your constant love and support.

Claire, my wife, my love, and best friend. I get to practice my questions on you every day.

Our daughters, Brooke and McKenzie. The answers you seek are in the questions you ask.

—Paul Cherry

ACKNOWLEDGMENTS

One of the blessings in life is to be able to publicly thank those who have contributed so much to your life's journey and direction. I want to thank Denita, my wife and fellow-adventurer, for enabling me to pursue my dreams of establishing businesses in Hong Kong and Singapore, even when that meant challenges and hardships for her. Our daughters—Kristin, Amber, Shanna, and Erin—are all women who consistently demonstrate what is really important and meaningful in life. They are "givers" and they ask hard and thought-provoking questions of themselves and others resulting, I believe, in making the world a better place.

Clarence Boland, Howard Davidson, United Methodist Bishop John Schol, and my close friend, Rev. Thomas Hall, all posed spiritually-based questions and I'll forever be grateful to them for their insights and guidance.

I have been blessed to have life work that has helped others live richer and fuller lives. Larry W. Dennis, my first sales trainer, and Ralph Nichols of the Ralph Nichols Corporation in Michigan were the first of many to provide support by guiding my career as they pushed me beyond my comfort zone with keen observations and questioning skills. My close friend, Dennis Deveja, has provided encouragement for me through the ups and downs of business initiatives and ventures. I was challenged to think globally by the late Dick Morgal, of Dale Carnegie and Associates, who motivated me to pursue my dreams globally. Ranjan Marwah, my first friend when moving to Hong Kong, asked the powerful "possibility" questions and stretched my thinking beyond what I thought possible.

Finally, I want to thank my parents-in-law, Frank and June Kohler. Even in their mid-eighties they continue to inspire me with their strong work ethic, persistence, and care for others. They've demonstrated the value of hard work, and June has shown me repeatedly that the best salesperson in the world is the one who really puts others first.

One can never say thank you to all who have contributed so much. There are many more. We have been given so much, blessed so much; we truly *stand on the shoulders of giants and warm ourselves at fires we did not build.* Thank you all.

—Patrick Connor

Index

Index

195

INDEX

Index

Index

Index

Success
  celebrating, 144–145
  creating, ix
  as an employee "want," 53, 63–69
  in family life, 182–190
  individual versus team, 20
  measures of, 121
  motivation and, 64–65, 69
Successful coaching, steps to, 44–48
Successful delegation, 37–38
Superior assessment, 157–160
Supervisors
  optimizing your relationship with, 116
  questions about, 172–173

Talent, tapping into, 28
Target reader, viii
Tasks, matching employees to, 31–32
Team achievement awards, 20
Team attitudes/actions, managing, 21–23
Team building, 16
Team-building exercises, 17
Team conflict, resolving, 16–21
Team cooperation, 16–17
Team dynamics, 26
Team goals, deciding on, 20
Team guidance, 13
Team health, sacrificing, 19–20
Team management, questions related to, 15–26
Team member activities, monitoring, 22
Team members, listening to, 22
"Team of the month" award, 20
Team performance, 15–16
Team problem solving, steps in, 18–19

Team productivity, improving, viii
Teams
  effective, ix
  making changes in, 23–26
  tuning in to, 22
Team strengths, playing to, 22
Techniques, revealing, 43
Teenagers
  communicating with, 186–187
  steps for listening to, 187–189
Thought processes, explaining, 108
Three-tier employee system, 95–96
Time, questions that save, 134–137
Time frame, questions to determine, 132
Top-tier employees, 96
Training, lack of, 57–58
Two-way communication, 125
  with bosses, 118

Unified team, creating, 20
Urgent issues, impact questions related to, 11

Vague questions, 3
Value, demonstrating, 144–145
Vendors, changing, 135–136
Volunteering, 158

"Want ads," for important positions, 72–74
Wants, conflicting, 150
Weathervane bosses, 116–117
Wickett, Michael, 93
Workplace atmosphere, poisoning, 64
Workplace interactions, ix
Workplace Internet access strategy, 63–64